# THE SCHOOL OF LOVE

## AND OTHER ESSAYS

# THE
# SCHOOL OF LOVE

## AND OTHER ESSAYS

BY THE MOST REVEREND

## ALBAN GOODIER, S.J.

ARCHBISHOP OF BOMBAY

AUTHOR OF
"THE PRINCE OF PEACE," "THE MEANING OF LIFE,"
"THE CROWN OF SORROW," ETC.

LONDON
BURNS OATES & WASHBOURNE LTD.
28 ORCHARD ST.          8–10 PATERNOSTER ROW
W. 1 ——————————————————————— E.C. 4
AND . AT . MANCHESTER . BIRMINGHAM . AND . GLASGOW
1926

*Made and Printed in Great Britain.*

Most of these essays have appeared in the
*Messenger of the Sacred Heart* for India.


St. Xavier's College,
Bombay,
*Feast of the Holy Name of Jesus,* 1918.

𝕹ihil 𝕺bstat.

INNOCENTIUS APAP, O P.

*Censor Deputatus.*

𝕴mprimatur.

EDM. CAN. SURMONT,

*Vicarius Generalis.*

WESTMONASTERII,
*die 14 Decembris,* 1919.

# CONTENTS

# THE SCHOOL OF LOVE
## AND OTHER ESSAYS

### LONELINESS

EVERY profession requires a special training; besides special powers and talents, besides special instruction, one may almost say it requires special virtues. The virtues most needful for a successful physician are not precisely those required for a successful lawyer; the one will have patience with the body of a man, the other will have patience with his ways. From both of these a soldier differs in almost every particular; perhaps he most of all needs patience with himself. The same is true of an apostle, of whatever kind he may be; he, too, must have his special qualifications. Priest or layman, religious or secular, man or woman, old or young, if God would make apostles of them, there is one school through which one and all must pass, one certificate they must all acquire; and when he is determined that they shall be apostles, he puts them through this school, whether they choose it or not.

And it is a school very different from that in which the world develops its ideal. When

1

it has the making of a man in hand, above all when it would make him one who is to understand and have influence over others, its first and foremost object is to give him what it calls experience of men. He is sent out to see the world, to mix with his fellow-men, to learn the art of dealing with them, of enjoying their company, of bending their lives; and it almost foretells the extent of his future plane of action by the measure of the knowledge he has gained.

Not so are the ways of God. He has other means of giving an apostle power over other men; indeed, it is the very opposite. "The weak things of this world God hath chosen to confound the strong," said the greatest of apostles; and by "the weak things" he meant not only the weakest instruments, but the methods that men most ignored. And of all methods perhaps none is more ignored by man as a race, and by man as an individual, than the method of loneliness. To most men loneliness is a doom. It is imposed upon a criminal as the heaviest of punishments; carried to extremes we know it will drive him mad; nothing seems so to unman a man as the loneliness of a prison cell. Even for those who are not criminals, nothing so wrings pity from a human heart as the sight of another who is utterly alone. Loneliness to many is the very ghost of life, dogging their steps, haunting them at every turn, from which they are always trying to escape. It cannot be fought, it cannot be avoided, yet there is nothing many more dread for themselves, or see with more concern in others.

Yet it is this very thing which God has chosen to be the school of training for His own. He has shown it without possibility of mistake. Look down the line of the Old Testament, and you will find it written everywhere. At this distance of time and space it is not easy for us to distinguish the details; we see in history the broad effects of lives, we do not always read between the lines and detect the causes which those effects imply. But we have only to hold our gaze steady, to wait for the haze to lift, and this detail at least will grow upon us. Abraham—what was he but a model of loneliness? "In those days God said to Abraham: Leave thy country and thy father's house and come into a land which I shall show thee." Moses, the saviour of his people, must first be brought up in an alien's house, and must then be made perfect in a wilderness. David was a lonely man. No otherwise could he have known the depth of soul that cried out in his lament for the loss of Saul and Jonathan; no otherwise could he have learnt to endure and love on when friend and foe alike turned against

him.  And the prophets, the giants of the
latter age, Amos and Osee, Isaias and Jere-
mias, Ezekiel and Daniel—what are they but
gaunt lonely figures, standing out upon the
distant sky-line, with the red light of a setting sun behind them?  Last of all comes
the Baptist, the man of all men lonely,
bestriding the gulf that separates two worlds,
who because of his momentous mission must
needs be alone from his childhood.

If in the days of God's manifest guidance
this is true, no less is it true in the days of
hidden grace.  Our Lord Himself was alone;
in the wilderness of humanity He lived, so
long a time, and men did not know Him.  He
was in the world, and the world knew Him
not; He came unto His own, and His own
received Him not.  His fellow-Nazarenes
claimed to know Him, and did not.  His
enemies knew Him and refused to own it.
His friends—at one point in His life "many
went back and walked no more with Him";
at another "all fled away"; at the very end
He had to say: "How long a time have I
been with you, and you have not known
me!"  He was born deserted, He lived alone,
He died a lonely criminal's death; and if we
want a proof that He felt it, we have it, first,
in His frequent cries of pain, and second, in
the eager way He grasped at and rewarded
every mark of companionship offered Him.

As with the Master so it was with the disciple. St. Paul's aloneness begins with his conversion; when he rose from his bed and his blindness God took him "into a silent place apart," to the desert of Arabia, and there He "spoke to his soul." And since his time, what has been the tale of every saint's life but one of a lonely heart, separated and hedged around, "a garden enclosed, a fountain sealed up," above all of such saints as were called to do a great life's work in the midst of men? We think of Cistercians and Carthusians, of Carmelites and Poor Clares, and fancy their lives are buried all alone in their cloisters; those who know have not very far to seek to find lonelier lives than theirs. Francis Xavier, to take but a single instance—how far more alone he stands, in the welter of human life in the midst of which he lived, than does St. Bruno himself on his lonely mountain-side!

So does God deal with His own, above all with those of His own whom He has chosen to use for others. And the reason is not hard to discover. There are three schools of suffering, each with its own special blessing to bestow—physical, mental, and that inner school which lies behind them both, loneliness of soul. Physical suffering makes for tenderness of heart and a patient judgment. Mental suffering gives a deepened sympathy, an active influence which when "lifted up draws all things to itself."

But loneliness of soul does more than this; it gives independence and strength. Even in the natural plane it secures liberty of spirit, it develops clearness of judgment, it enforces power of will. But this is by no means all. In the Old Testament Wisdom is heard to say: "Come with me into a silent place apart, and I will speak to thy soul;" and no one who has heard the calling of the Holy Spirit can misunderstand what this means— the deafness to His voice that may be caused by the din of men, and the clear ring that is given to His words when they come to us across the desert through the night. Loneliness of soul gives wisdom—that breadth of vision that belongs to him who sees all the valley from the hill-top. Loneliness of soul gives understanding—that further power of seeing beneath the surfaces of life. Loneliness of soul gives counsel to sustain another, and fortitude to endure its own burthen; all the seven gifts of the Holy Ghost come through and are fostered by loneliness of soul.

These are some of the fruits of this special school of suffering. None the less, let it not be forgotten that a school of suffering it is. We are not speaking here of the loneliness which is a joy and a comfort, in which, as the popular phrase goes, one is "never less alone than when alone"; we are speaking of that sense of desertion, of alienation from one's kindred, of being somehow out of joint with all the world, of separation from God Himself, which human nature can scarcely endure; which even our Lord Himself considered to justify a cry for relief. Physical suffering He foresaw for His disciples, but He merely bade them rejoice at the prospect. Mental suffering He also promised them; this, again, they were to take as a sign that His blessing was upon them. But loneliness of soul He treats quite differently. Its agony He fully recognises; He is not afraid to let them see its effect upon Himself. In the Garden, on the Cross, His cries had almost scandalised posterity. And as for His whole life—an angel lost and broken-winged in this poor world would be a pitiable, lonely thing; what then must have been the loneliness of the exiled Son of God?

Then, having "given us an example," having justified, as it were, our complainings by His own, He proceeds to soothe the bitterness for those who must needs undergo it. "My little children," He calls them, on the eve of the great Day of Loneliness. "Let not your heart be troubled," He says, "nor let it be afraid. . . . It is expedient for you that I go, for if I go not the Spirit will not

come to you;" and He bribes them to go
through with it because of all that is to follow. Last of all, He assures them that it
will not be all desertion: "I will not leave
you orphans; I will come to you. Now
indeed you have sorrow, but I will see you
again, and your heart shall rejoice; and your
joy no man shall take from you." Then, as
if to support Himself by the same argument
by which He supports them, He concludes:
"Behold the hour cometh, and it is now
come, that you shall be scattered every man
to his own, and shall leave me alone: and yet
I am not alone, because the Father is with me."

Nowhere has Christ our Lord come nearer
to us than in His loneliness and ours.
Nowhere has He shown Himself more human.
Nowhere has He more condoned the cry of
pain, the appeal for some relief; nowhere has
He done more, by example and by promise,
to nerve us to endurance. And the truth of
His promise who that has tried does not
know? St. Paul speaks for such as these,
and they echo his words which have for them
a meaning all their own: "I am sure that
neither death, nor life, nor Angels, nor principalities, nor powers, nor things present, nor
things to come, nor might, nor height, nor
depth, nor any other creature shall be able
to separate me from the love of God, which
is in Christ Jesus our Lord."

# CRAVINGS

THERE is one characteristic common to all great souls, whether they be good or evil, in whatever sphere they may be found. It is seen in a Byron, or a Shelley, or a Goethe, in an Alexander, a Cæsar, a Napoleon, in a Luther, a Calvin, a Wesley, in a Paul, a Xavier, a Teresa. In some it attains to some issue, though never to a complete satisfaction; in others it seems only to add to the tragedy of life, rendering it broken-winged and desperate. This common characteristic is a certain craving to be something more than merely ordinary, to do something more than it is given to everyone to do, to attain to some end above the common; this alone seems to them to justify life. As Browning has put it—

> " A man's reach should be beyond his grasp,
>   Or what's a Heaven for ?"

One man will endeavour to satisfy this craving in words. He will dive through life itself and fathom its depths; he will disclose its pearls or its weeds as the case may be; such a man we call either a poet or a philosopher, or both. Another will express it in action. He will set out to conquer nations

9

or to govern them: he will make himself a leader of men for good or for evil; such we call a general or a statesman. A third is roused to remedy the evils of his time, whether they be real or imagined, religious, or political, or social. He forms his theory, he has his own end in view, he multiplies his following; for good or for evil, his mark on the world is permanent. Such a man we call a reformer, or a revolutionist, as the case may be. Yet a fourth is filled with a craving for that which no deed, or triumph, or reform in the world can give him. He hungers for that which is beyond the world's edge; he must leap out to it, grasp it, and live the life of man towards it; for this end every sacrifice in this world is a negligible quantity. Such a man we call a saint, at least such are the foundations of a saint, and it is on this account that the saints are the greatest among mankind.

They are, we assert, the greatest men among mankind, even judged by man's own standards. For if greatness consists in the violence of one's craving, the object towards which it tends, and the force with which it is followed, then do the saints compare with and surpass all the greatest heroes in the world. In other men the range is avowedly confined to this life and all that it contains; for them the horizon loses itself in the mist

of the infinite, their aspirations are infinite in
range, infinite in possibilities, and therefore
beyond the power of eye to see, or ear to
hear, or the heart of man to conceive. Others
have human ends, they make use of human
means; these make light of what is human,
they take its effects as but the by-product of
their labour, and for the means, they "have
nothing and possess all things," "glory in
their infirmities that the power of God may
be manifested in them," take it as their principle that "the weak things of this world
hath God chosen to confound the strong."

Thus is this almost infinite craving an
essential characteristic of sanctity; without
it a man would not rise above this world,
with it he becomes the greatest among men.
It has two necessary consequences; it
explains that paradox, that consciousness at
once of success and failure, which seems to
run through the lives of all the saints, and
indeed of all who, though not saints, nevertheless aspire after sanctity. Their cravings
make them do greater things than it is given
to less hungry hearts to do; these same cravings make them dissatisfied with all that they
have done, so that in the end they can only
cry out: "I am a useless servant!" The
humility of the saint, such a contradiction to
those who look on from the outside, is no
contradiction in itself; it is only a recognition

of the vast difference between all that he accomplishes and the glorious ideal which he has before him. Let us look at this a little more closely, for it touches perhaps the darkest spot in the lives of many.

It is of the essence of growth of any kind, to become disillusioned. A child is delighted with its toys; it grows, and immediately discards them; it has been disillusioned. A boy or girl revels in a certain kind of story; they grow, and tend to pity those who understand no more. A youth is keen to excel in sport or games; he grows, and only the battlefield or the government of men will satisfy him. And with the spiritual-minded man it is the same. He may have revelled in the enjoyment of this life, and even for a time have found it sufficient. But one day he begins to grow. He discovers there are more things in heaven and earth, than are dreamt of in this world's philosophy. His knowledge of the more and greater things creates some disgust for the little things around him with which, nevertheless, so long as he lives, his life must be filled up. He is a little disillusioned, exactly as the child, the boy, the youth; and the consequent sense of disappointment, or failure, he may easily take for more than he should.

Again, the spiritual-minded man cannot but be of an ardent nature. Keen to appreciate, he is also keen to love; and, while he grows, until his love has found its final goal, he will more than once experience the disillusion of love that has been ill-bestowed. He will bestow it where it is not deserved, deceived by some little outward show. He will give it and it will not be returned. He will pour it out, and will find that the cup that should have received it, could hold so much and no more. And meanwhile his own heart will be growing; it will yearn for something more worthy, for the best thing that may be loved; it will reach out into the infinite, both of giving and of receiving. When it has gone thus far, when it has drunk of the best and worthiest that this life has to give, and has found it wanting, when more is not received, when the little that it had is taken away, by death, by separation, by faithlessness, by misunderstanding, by whatever cause, when the ordinary interests of flattened-out life absorb its time and powers, but have no place for the affections, there grows a sense of loss, of disappointment, which the hungry victim may too often mistake for failure.

Or thirdly, there is the result of that reaction which comes from experience; and this is of two kinds. There is the bitter discovery that men and things are not always the ideals that he had pictured in his mind.

This world, and every man in this world, is capable of so much, might be so much, if only——! And the "if only" is frustrated by so many trifles, or else, apparently, by so much that God, if He would, could arrange! Sometimes individuals will not see what is good, sometimes seeing they will not follow; sometimes a good thing, to us so clear, is contested, opposed, thwarted by others, apparently no less eager than ourselves in the service of God; sometimes it is circumstances that hinder any possibility of action; sometimes it is those in authority who seem to hinder. Sometimes there is actual scandal and corruption where nothing but zeal and sacrifice should reign. In a thousand ways we "live and learn"; and it needs a patient and a persevering heart to endure loyal under the process. It begins to suspect its own cravings; perhaps it begins to resign itself to a lower satisfaction.

The second kind is the experience of ourselves. From time to time in our lives the supernatural gains a strong hold upon us. There are periods, longer or shorter, for which we can account or cannot, when we seem to awaken to a new revelation; when we see things we never saw before, when prayer becomes on a sudden a new light, at once satisfying and easy, when effort after nobler life is full of inspiration, when we scarcely touch the ground beneath us on our way to God, when we tell ourselves, with some enthusiasm, that now " we have found Him whom our soul loveth, we have held Him and will not let Him go"; that henceforth "nothing shall separate us from the love which we have in Christ Jesus Our Lord." Then on a sudden, or perhaps it may be gradually, all this passes away. The revelation grows dim in the distance, remaining as a recollection and no more; prayer becomes again the humdrum affair it was of old, if it does not sink even lower; effort becomes impossible, progress is none, the burden of this life and its myriad temptations presses on us, we walk with leaden shackles on our feet.

At once we are troubled and distressed. We compare our present state with our last and discover what we call a falling off. We cannot help making the contrast, and it needs both effort and understanding not to draw a seemingly obvious conclusion. If once we prayed well, and now the least prayer is a weary labour, we presume that this proves our own shortcomings. If before we could record daily victories, and now we have nothing but defeats, this we take as clear evidence that we are wholly wanting. If now we are obsessed on every side with temptations of every nature, and once we had sailed into the open sea with nothing but a straight course before us, we tell ourselves that we have gone back. Our heart becomes more hungry than ever. Having once tasted "how sweet is the Lord," it can never be satisfied with anything less; and it takes its dissatisfaction for an evil sign.

In reality it is the opposite. A hungry heart is, as we have said, the foundation of a saintly heart; it is the heart that is settled and contented, that kills its cravings and satisfies its hunger with the husks that lie about, it is such a heart that should make us uneasy. And God so loves a hungry heart that He will stir the hunger in a hundred ways. One of these is to give it just a taste of "the things that are more excellent," and then to take them away. Let us not be mistaken; let us not misinterpret ourselves; let us rejoice that we are made so to "hunger and thirst after justice, for we shall have our fill!"

# PRAYER

A CHILD never complains of being unable to pray; complaints are seldom made by older people to whom prayer is not an ordinary thing or a well-known experience; it is only those who have learnt something of the meaning and life of prayer that complain of the difficulty they find in it. One might almost go further and assert the seeming paradox that the more we know about prayer, the more difficult it tends to become.

Of course, prayer is a gift of God, and His gifts are free from His hand and may not be purchased. Nevertheless of all His gifts perhaps none is more nearly purchasable than prayer; none, that is to say, which He more willingly gives in return for what we offer Him. More than any other of His gifts that of prayer depends on our desire for it, our efforts to attain it, and the dispositions we prepare for its reception.

Hence, while we must allow that God can and often does bestow the gift of prayer, and consolation in prayer, and life in prayer, of His own overflowing bounty and without consideration of previous dispositions, still it is also true that ordinarily, and ultimately for

17                                              2

all, certain dispositions must always be pre-
served if the habit of, and interest in, and
relish for prayer are to be maintained.
Prayer is a delicate flower needing to be
guarded and tended; if we would have it in
full bloom we must look well to it, both in
its growth and in its hey-day, and in all its
surroundings.   What, then, are some at least
of the precautions we should take?  They are
best learnt by each one from his own personal experience; there is no other road to
prayer; not what we have read in books, or
what we have heard from others, but exactly
as much as we have learnt from ourselves
and no more.

Here at least may be suggested a few pre-
liminary warnings.  When we examine our
prayer or our failure in it, the first thing we
usually have to say is that our minds have
been far afield.  We began well enough—or
we did not, which is much more common than
we are always willing to allow—but almost
immediately we were lost.  People we know
wandered through our brain, above all two
classes; those we like best and those we like
least.  With the former we built our castles
in the clouds; the latter we pelted with torrents of abuse, and saw ourselves in imagination triumphantly stamping on their prostrate
forms; or events of the past, or imaginary
events of the future, turned themselves over

and over, distorted themselves, mixed themselves up, and usually left us either humbled at our proneness to evil, or grumbling at somebody's imagined injustice towards us. Let us humbly confess it; this or such as this is often the sum total of our morning meditation.

Or, secondly, we find we have taken up a restful position of body. We are rather more than usually tired—how many mornings are we not able to say this! We are afraid of straining ourselves by a long vigil, we recall the warning of St. Teresa that no one can pray whose body is in torture. Besides we have so often found, or at least we tell ourselves that we have often found, that a restful attitude conduces to prayer. But as a matter of fact, whatever may be the prayer of the first half-minute, the restful attitude has led to an absolute blank; it has either soothed us into slumber or else has let our minds go wandering away to the moon. The end comes, and we find ourselves, in body, and mind, and soul, exactly where we were when we sat down or reclined. Of how many morning meditations is this the history?

There is yet a third experience. It often happens that much as we desire and relish the thought of spiritual things at other times, in time of prayer this desire and this relish seem utterly to vanish. There succeeds nothing but weariness and languor; mean and shameful thoughts come careering through our brain which at other times are wholly absent; and we have scarcely begun our prayer, but we long with an almost irresistible longing for the end. Any distraction becomes welcome, any excuse for limiting the time allotted is acceptable; instead of being the desire of our hearts, the time of prayer becomes the time of almost intolerable torture.

These are three common experiences, which are perhaps the tale of the prayer of many, and from which very few indeed escape. But fortunately they have their remedy written right across them; we have but to acknowledge them, to discover the right relation that exists between prayer and mortification, that to some extent at least the one is the price of the other, and how far and in what coin that price must be paid.

For in the first place if excessive preoccupation is a hindrance to prayer, then we must train ourselves, especially before the time of prayer, to resist this preoccupation. This does not, or at least need not, mean that we must do less work than before, or that we must be less interested in it, or that we must pay less attention to it than to ourselves; the example of all the saints of prayer, witness St. Francis Xavier, St. Teresa, St. Vincent de Paul, is evidence in abundance that prayer never hinders work. But it does mean that no matter how much, or how engrossing, or how urgent the work may be, it must never be allowed to master us. We must never let ourselves become the slaves of our surroundings or our circumstances. We must educate the mind by severe discipline, if necessary say to everything that threatens to engross and overwhelm us: "Thus far and no further." It must learn to shut the door to interference, to preserve its command of its own castle; this is the active side of the virtue known as peace of mind, and such discipline, such mortification, will teach us to command our thoughts and affections in time of prayer.

Secondly, if bodily ease is found, after an honest self-examination, to be a hindrance to prayer, then not in time of prayer only but at other times also we must train the body to give up its comfort for the sake of energy of mind and heart. It is not enough to wait till the time of prayer comes in order to begin our educating of the body; then, not only are the reasons for relaxation more urgent and apparent, but the habit of always yielding tells heavily against us. Lazy-bodied people at ordinary times have no sufficient vigour with which to resist laziness of body in time of prayer. On the other hand a little sacrifice at other times, gradual inuring of ourselves not to have absolutely all the comfort that our bodies seek, reacts in prayer and gives us the physical strength to resist this second hindrance.

Thirdly, if, as we have said, nature resists the supernatural effort to be made in prayer, if prayer time is a time of weariness and agony, then there are three things to be done; for, be it noticed, this is a hindrance to prayer much more likely to come from without than from within, much more likely to be a real trial than merely a consequence of our own unfaithfulness and self-indulgence. First of all at other times, which are not strictly times of prayer, when the spirit is moved to pray, to utter an ejaculation, to answer the ringing of the Angelus, to pay a visit to the Blessed Sacrament, let it not be too easily thwarted. Let it be allowed to pray when nature does not seem to be in conflict; gradually nature itself will learn to "taste and see how sweet is the Lord."

Again, when prayer is irksome, when body and soul are weary, then, if prayer is not a matter of duty, it is of little use driving the soul against its own inclination. To pray long at such times, simply because one has made up one's mind to do so, does but make prayer a matter of greater horror; and this warning we have from perhaps the greatest student of the human soul, St. Ignatius Loyola. Long devotions at such times, car-

ried out because they are long, may easily
break the spirit and turn it away from prayer
altogether.

On the other hand, when prayer is of duty,
when the prayers we say are those which belong to our state of life or are appointed by our
rule, our practice must be the exact opposite.
We must then not clip the time, but we must
train ourselves to prolong it; and the reason
is that prayer is then something more than a
matter of inclination. It is the fulfilment of
a duty; and no yielding in duty can possibly
make for growth in prayer.

These then are three common hindrances to
prayer, very often overlooked, and yet stunt-
ing prayer at its outset; and these are three
remedies by which they may be met. Of
course it may be, and for the fervent it often
is, that apparent failure in prayer is due to
other causes. With all the best will and
effort and preparation in the world we may
still seem to make little progress; the trial
may come entirely from the hand of God.
Nevertheless it is possible that even this may
depend upon the shortcomings of which we
have spoken far more than we at first suspect; we may be making many efforts in many
ways, and yet in some conscious particular we
may know that we are wholly yielding to ourselves. In any case we can go no further
until the first evils have been cured; and in

matter of fact God always in the end, or from time to time, rewards and encourages consistent effort enough and more than enough to make us feel that it has been worth while.

Hence to sum up the duty of the man of prayer: discipline or control of thought, discipline or control of body, discipline or control of nature. One might well add a fourth which might be called discipline of heart; for here, too, is a serious, even a fatal hindrance to prayer. We do not like to own it; we scarcely have the courage to face the consequence; still a disordered affection, a giving too much of oneself to any creature whatsoever, a caring too much for anyone or anything, is often a cause of failure in prayer which would otherwise be good. Human nature refuses to acknowledge it; it looks for any other cause; it will even ascribe it to its own wickedness; but if we would learn to pray we must be quite true to ourselves and in this matter most of all.

# SOME HINTS ON PRAYER

## I

St. Teresa and St. John of the Cross, the great teachers of prayer in more recent times, both of them lament, not so much that people do not pray more, but that they do not make more advancement in prayer. They tell us very plainly that prayer is a science as well as a practice; that if we will only go the right way about it we shall learn astonishingly both what prayer itself is, and what wonderful things it has to reveal, and that there is no one, man or woman, educated or uneducated, religious or secular, but can come to at least some knowledge, much more than most of us usually achieve. But, alas! they add, there are few who make much advancement; few get beyond the most elementary principles; and the chief reasons are either that they will not persevere, or that they fear to let themselves go forward, or that they have no one to show them the way to proceed.

Now it is not for anyone to presume to set himself up as a guide in prayer, much less as a universal guide; for prayer is an individual thing, it is the individual's intercourse with God, and God has His own way of dealing with individuals. Nevertheless there are certain elementary truths, not realised by all, yet easily discovered by one who has had much to do with prayer, whether in his own soul or in others; truths which, if once accepted, will at once clear away many obstacles for any soul that wishes to progress in prayer. To mention a few of these may be useful; it may give a little light to some who walk in darkness, and who may already have begun to despond about their prayer, finding as no doubt they do that it falls so short of their desires and ambitions, finding it so disappointing.

In the first place, then, let it be remembered that prayer does not consist in merely saying prayers. Prayer, from its definition, is "the raising of the mind and heart to God"; and there are many more ways, sometimes better ways, of doing this than by repeating forms of prayer however good. Forms of prayer are good in so far as they do this for us and no further; they help us to put into words the thoughts of our mind and the feelings of our heart; but if those thoughts and feelings can be taught to express themselves spontaneously, even without any words at all or at least with very few, then our prayer is better than that which depends upon a form.

"But I am afraid to give up the form. That at least ties me down to something clear and definite. If I gave up the form, and trusted to my own thoughts and feelings and expression, these may some day fail me, and then I should be without any prayer at all." This objection is a good one; a proof that it is a good one is that it is very common, very real, and obviously comes from those who wish to do their best. Still it is an objection and no more, and is one of the chief hindrances to progress in prayer.

For clearly what is one's own is better than what we substitute in its place; even if our words are more faulty, or our expression more vague, what comes hot from the heart is better than all else. When we read the New Testament, and hear the poor man on the roadside merely crying: "Lord, help me!" or St. Peter breaking down with: "Lord, thou knowest that I love thee;" or St. Thomas paralysed into his: "My Lord, and my God!" or Our Lord Jesus Himself unable to do more than repeat "the self-same words: Father, if it be possible, let this chalice pass from me;" then we know that we are listening to the truest prayer. And when in like manner in our own turn we find our own hearts crying out to God, whether in faith, or love, or hope, or contrition, or oblation, or anything else, then we should know that our prayer is of our best, even a minute of which crying is more precious than another prayer of many words.

The first hint, then, to be given to one who

would make progress in prayer is that the soul should not confine itself so as to be tied down to a formula however good. Suppose, for example, that I am accustomed to take a quarter of an hour, in preparation for or thanksgiving after Communion; and suppose that to fill up this time I have a fixed set of prayers which I repeat. I may some day find, and if I try I most certainly shall find, that while repeating the prayers, or even before, I am impelled to dwell on one word, or one idea, or one strong feeling of the heart; I am drawn to say " Jesus!" in welcome, and to dwell upon the name, or to be sorry that I receive Him so poorly, or whatever else; shall I entertain this feeling at the expense of my set of prayers, or must I keep my rule and say them ?

The answer should be clear; keep the time, not the form of words; if I speak heart to heart with God even for two minutes my prayer is deeper, and will tell more deeply on me, than the words of another; and I shall learn soon how from that small beginning God will draw me forward and teach me more. If I am true to the appointed time I need not fear the danger that the objection suggests; and when I find that my mind wanders, or my heart is cold and unmoved, then I can always fall back upon my set prayers to fill up the time that remains.

Only let us be simple and genuine in our prayer, and we shall soon discover the value of this "liberty of the children of God"; for forms of prayer, excellent and constantly useful as they are, are best when they suggest this deeper praying of our own, not when they chain us down to their repetition. Even the best prayers, if merely repeated and not delayed upon, will in time become a weary formula; and which of us has not gone through the experience of out-growing some form of prayer, and yet sometimes we are afraid to set it aside? But such prayerfulness as is here suggested is always alive; and if the form is in consequence less often said, it has given way to something far more fruitful. I would rather say, "Jesus, I love you," for an hour, if I could mean it all the time, than repeat or read the most perfect act of love composed by the greatest saint or the most consummate poet. My words would be fewer, and weaker, and more stammering; but Jesus would know that at least they are mine and no other's, the words of

> "An infant crying in the night,
> An infant crying for the light,
> And with no language but a cry;"

and I think He would hear them more tenderly.

Hence the first practical hint to be given to one who sincerely wishes to learn how to pray

is that we should be faithful to our time of
prayer rather than to our words.   Prayer cannot easily be measured by words; it is
measured best by earnestness of purpose,
depth of meaning, and intensity of feeling;
and by feeling is not meant our sentiment, but
the reality behind it that abides in the heart.
This is the method by which, on his own confession, St. Aloysius Gonzaga grew to be so
great a man of prayer; he began with the
form, like the rest of us, gradually the form
was made to yield to the feelings of his heart
which it evoked, in the end we find him writ-
ing and developing forms of his own.

And the same may be said of many others,
conspicuous saints of prayer on the one hand,
and on the other hidden souls of prayer who
know God and His Christ by an intimate
experience all their own.   Let us take an
example.   Not so long ago a certain lady,
who gave much of her time and her wealth to
the poor, chanced in her rounds to come
across an old woman in a humble cottage, who
had been bed-ridden for years.   She sat by the
sufferer's side, gave her what comfort she
could, and then asked her about her prayers.

" Do you say your rosary every day ?" she
asked.

" Every day ?   Bless you no, not every day,
Madame; I haven't always time," was the
answer.

Not always time!  And yet the old woman was lying there all day long and every day, often with no one to visit her for hours together!

"Why, what do you do with your time?" the lady naturally asked.

"Well, Madame," said the poor victim; "when I first broke my thigh and was told I should never rise from my bed again, I just thought I would give myself to my prayers. So I arranged some prayers that I would say every day, and some I would say at intervals; and to make them go better I would say them very slowly.  But soon the 'Our Father' began to grow and grow, until now it sometimes takes me the whole week to get through it.  Oh, Madame, if people only knew what was in the 'Our Father'!"

And here the poor, uneducated old woman broke into an exposition of the prayer, the nature of the Fatherhood of God and His attitude to us His children, such, as the lady herself told me, as might have come from the lips of the most highly trained saint and theologian.

And perhaps they did; but from a saint and theologian trained in God's own school, the school of prayer combined with welcome suffering.  Which, incidentally, reminds us of two other truths: first, that suffering is not wholly evil, however much we may fear it; and second, that prayer and suffering are seldom far removed, but that both give strength, and depth, and fruitfulness to one another.

# SOME HINTS ON PRAYER

## II

IN our last essay on this subject we made an attempt to let souls understand that often enough the chief hindrance to progress in prayer is just our own way of praying; we cling sometimes too much to our adopted forms of prayer, good as they are in themselves, and so chain down the mind and heart, preventing them from raising themselves spontaneously to God. Let it never be forgotten that spontaneous prayer, straight from the heart, however feebly it be worded, is always better than prayer of form, and is always likely to lead to higher things. Fixed forms are good, and are even necessary, because often enough the soul is unable to express itself; but when it can express itself, then let it do so, speaking to God face to face so far as it is permitted.

We come now to a second consideration which naturally follows from the first, and it is this: If our own expression of our hearts in prayer is better than any other, and if our own expression of ourselves never wears out or becomes a mere form whereas other kinds, however good, are liable to be outgrown, it becomes important that the soul should train itself in self-expression in prayer, so that sufficient words may come spontaneously to it. This is one of the great values of ejaculatory prayers, and of short phrases from the Scripture, such as " My Lord and my God," " Jesus, Son of David, have mercy on me," " For thou, O Lord, art sweet and gentle, and of much mercy to all who hope in thee," "Lord, thou knowest all things, thou knowest that I love thee;" phrases such as these crystallise our thoughts, and the heart when it endeavours to leap up to God finds in them an easy and spontaneous form of speech. These, then, should be collected and often used; and there is no man or woman in the world, however "unspiritual," however preoccupied with business, but can practise this method, anywhere, everywhere, and realise its benefit.

For some, indeed, this form of prayer, once adopted, abundantly suffices; it leads of itself to almost everything else. For others it is easier to train the soul in self-expression by means of definite acts—of faith: "Lord, I believe, help my unbelief;" of hope: "In thee, O Lord, I have hoped, let me not be confounded for ever;" of humility: "Lord, I am not worthy that thou shouldst enter under my roof;" of contrition: "Father, I have sinned against heaven and before thee;" and so on.

This method is usually better than the last, chiefly because there is less danger of wandering, one act naturally leading to another.

But that this form of prayer may be made most fruitfully, it is always well that some plan be made beforehand of the road we propose to follow. Thus, before Communion, one may say to oneself: "To-day I will exercise myself in Faith, Hope and Charity;" in a visit to the Blessed Sacrament one may propose: "I will make Acts of Humility, Contrition, and Love in His Presence;" on a journey, in a tram-car, during an empty ten minutes, one may begin: "I will make an act of the presence of God to me, and of my presence to Him, and let my heart speak to Him as my companion." We need not always keep to the arrangement; but such preparation as this is splendid training, not only for prayer, but also in the all-important matter of self-control in all things.

Still there are some with whom even this form of prayer will not always be satisfying. There come times when no outward words will sufficiently express the depth of feeling in the soul; it must speak for itself or not at all. Especially is this the case when one is impressed with the sense of one's own nothingness, or when the misery of sin, especially of one's own sins, is deeply realised, or again, as a reaction to, or consequence of this, when one yearns towards a better way of living, greater truth and greater self-surrender.

To such one can only suggest a kind of prayer, a model upon which the soul may work for itself, climbing to God by means of a ladder of its own making. The method is to hold its thoughts steady, taking one at a time without confusion, letting one lead to another naturally, and as slowly as the soul will go, that it may draw from each step all the fruit that it may be able.

As an example, let us take a prayer of appeal to Our Lady. The soul comes into her presence. It is conscious of her, conscious of itself, conscious also of the hunger that is gnawing at its heart. Then spontaneously the expressions come, one succeeding the other, very slowly but very easily, crystallising each new feeling as it takes form, and holding it till the soul is satisfied. In this way the prayer may take some such shape as the following:

### A Visit to Our Lady

Mary, full of grace,
Mary, Mother of God,
Mary, my Mother,
You are God's perfect creature,
You know me well,
And love me very fondly,
As a mother her most sickly child,
As a mother her most wayward child,

I am weak and sickly,
I am self-willed and wayward,
I want to do better,
I want to be true,
Of myself I am unable,
My wilfulness is too much for me,
My circumstances beat me,
You want to help me, I know,
And you are able,
What, then, prevents you?
Is it anything in myself?
It can be nothing in you.
But what can I do?
I cannot mend myself,
Do it for me,
Take away what hinders you.
I am sincere,
If I am not I want to be,
Take me at my word,
Be a mother to me,
Firmly but gently,
Let me see truly,
Make me be true,
Make me act truly,
Make me worthy of you;

and the prayer will then conclude with a Hail
Mary, a Salve Regina, or any other form of
prayer according to the choice of the soul.

Or again one may thus draw out a visit to
the Blessed Sacrament.  One comes into the

presence of Our Lord.   One realises Him, one
realises oneself, one has in mind what it is one
wishes to express; and the prayer may take a
form such as this:

### A Visit to the Blessed Sacrament

Jesus,
Jesus Christ,
Jesus, Son of God,
Jesus, God made Man,
Jesus, truly man,
Jesus, with a greatly loving Heart,
Jesus, here present,
You are,
You love me,
You have proved it wonderfully,
In your own life and in mine,
In ways I know,
In ways I do not know;
I am a poor creature,
I have done endless harm,
I have hurt you,
I am sorry,
I would do better,
But I cannot trust myself,
I seem incapable of any good,
And yet you want me
To be yours, live with you,
Work with you, die with you,
You know I cannot of myself,
I cannot keep from hurting you,

Yet you pity me, love me,
Even me,
And you have chosen even me,
Then I rely on you,
I have no other help,
Keep me from doing evil,
Keep me from hurting you,
Make me true in myself,
Make me true to you,
You can if you will,
And if I will,
And I do will so far as I am able,
I have no other hope,
I give you myself,
In spite of, against, my own opposition;

and the prayer may fitly conclude with the *Anima Christi*, or any other form of prayer which the soul prefers.

The length of time such a prayer will take is quite indefinite. At one time, when the soul is sluggish or distracted, or when the body is weary, it may be short, at another time it may easily expand into an hour; in either case the effort should be made to be very real, to mean exactly what we say, to delay until we are sure that we mean it, speaking to Our Lady or Our Lord directly, as to a personal friend in whose presence we are. If this is done it will soon be found that many more steps can be made between those here suggested, each soul hav-

ing its own particular thoughts, reflections
and manners of expressing its love and contrition.

Such prayer is among the most satisfying
to the human soul, and is far easier than those
think who have not tried it. But who has not
tried it, however unconsciously? For who
has not striven at some time to utter to
God his soul exactly as it is, and what is the
prayer here suggested but this? Let us bear
in mind the words of a great saint of prayer:
"It is not abundance of knowledge that satisfies the soul, but to feel and relish things
internally."

# SOME HINTS ON PRAYER

## III

As a result of the remarks made in our last instruction on Prayer not a few have expressed a desire to see more illustrations of the method of prayer that is there advocated. We proceed then to give further examples, but with a word of warning. Let it be remembered that they are examples and no more. They are not "prayers" in the commonly accepted sense; they are not given merely to be read. They are an effort to show how the soul may guide itself in prayer; how much prayer may be expressed in few words; they are simply a suggestion of the way a soul may, as it were, steady itself in its upward flight.

Two illustrations of this method of prayer have been given, one to Our Lady, the other to Jesus Christ Our Lord; we proceed to give another addressed to the first Person of the Blessed Trinity, to whom after some experience it is always most easy to pray.

A Prayer to God the Father

My Father,
You are so great,
I am so little,

You are the First and the Last,
The Beginning and the End,
Almighty, Everlasting,
And yet my Father,
You made me,
The creature that I am,
With my powers, my weaknesses,
Because you wanted me,
Even me,
You put me here,
You gave me this state of life,
You want me back,
I want to be yours,
I want to do your work,
When the end comes I want to go to you,
But without you I cannot,
You will not fail me,
You cannot fail me,
Let me not fail you.
I know my weakness,
I have learnt it from my falls,
Which you have permitted,
That I might learn,
Is it necessary to be taught more?
I can do nothing of myself,
I cannot desire to do anything,
I cannot keep from harm,
I cannot want to keep from harm,
Help me that I may,
Help me that I may desire it,
Give me the desire of sacrifice,

At least the desire of the desire,
I am an infant asking for bread,
Will my Father give me a stone?

The prayer concludes very naturally with the
"Our Father"; which of itself, treated in a
manner like the above, may easily "raise the
mind and heart to God" for an hour.

The next illustration is a prayer to the Third
Person of the Blessed Trinity; again a very
easy prayer to one who has learnt devotion
to God the Holy Ghost.

### A Prayer to God the Holy Ghost

Holy Spirit of God,
Love of God,
Silent, secret, all preserving,
Breathing where you list,
Expressing our longings,
You are wisdom,
You are love,
You are strength and fidelity,
I am none of these,
I need them all,
Sincerely I want them,
I do believe sincerely I want them,
You are the Father of the poor,
You do not fail,
Will you fail me?
That I may never fail you,
I cannot trust myself,

That I may never do wrong,
That I may be wise,
According to my place in life,
That I may love,
Truly, not falsely,
That I may be faithful,
To God, to men,
That I may have strength,
Sufficient for the task you give me,
And may use it.

Let the prayer conclude with the "Veni Creator Spiritus," or even better with the "Veni Sancte Spiritus," since the latter, line by line, suggests a continuation of the same simple method.

Lastly, as an example of the way the method may be applied to any of the saints, we may take a prayer to St. Joseph.

### A Prayer to St. Joseph

St. Joseph,
The "just man,"
The perfect man of Nazareth,
The Spouse of Mary,
The Foster-father of Jesus,
The Patron of labour,
The Patron of a happy death,
The Patron of the whole Church,
Sinless,
Selfless,

Unflinchingly generous,
I am a poor beggar,
I am in need,
My tale is against me,
I am very disappointing,
I have no excuse,
I deserve nothing,
Even for the future, how much can I
    promise?
I cannot be sure of myself,
But I would it were otherwise,
I would become true,
And you can help me,
For Jesus hears you,
Ask him to forgive,
Ask Him to forget,
Ask Him to make me sinless,
Like to yourself,
To make me selfless,
Like yourself,
To make me generous,
Take me as your companion,
And Mary's,
And His.

These examples will suffice to show how the mind may be trained to make its own way in prayer. In general one may notice that the plan is in each case much the same; indeed this plan lies at the root of all prayer of colloquy. First comes a realisation of the person to whom we pray, with whatever expressions of affection it may evoke; then a realisation of oneself in contrast with this person, with the necessary acts of humility and contrition, or of love and hope; finally, and spontaneously, there is that appeal from one in need to one who possesses an abundance, inspired by a mutual affection which knows it can presume to ask. Let the actual words be of least account. The realisation is the all-important matter; when, with a single, selfless, unaffected heart we forget to watch our thoughts and words, then the thoughts and words will come of themselves, spontaneously and hot from the heart.

This last remark suggests a word of warning. We are told by saints who knew much about prayer that we should examine our prayer and see if we can what makes us fail. This is very sound advice; no matter what hints may be suggested for prayer, the soundest hint is that we should study our own soul, find the way that it finds easiest and best, and cultivate that as well as we are able. St. Teresa encourages this method; so do many modern teachers of prayer.

At the same time, during the hour of prayer itself, there is no distraction more fatal than to reflect and ask oneself whether one is praying well or not. Such a process is often mere vanity, and vanity is the ruin of all prayer. It kills spontaneity, it stifles fervour, it puts a veil between oneself and God; it may even substitute oneself and one's own image in the place of Him to whom we wish to pray. Let preparation for prayer be as careful as we like; after prayer let us ask ourselves what has helped us most, and what has been a hindrance. But during prayer let there be nothing between the heart and God. The great effort of the soul should be to realisation of the truth; and this, if gained even for a moment, as St. Teresa very well says, is worth all the pains that may be taken, and bears fruit in great peace of mind.

One last remark may be made in regard to the attitude to prayer. It is said of St. Ignatius Loyola that during his busy day he had little time for long prayer, but that he would find satisfaction in a few moments here and there, whether in his room or before the Blessed Sacrament. But even for these few moments he would pause before he began; he would not plunge into even so short a prayer without some kind of preparation, some thought of what he was about to do and how he was about to do it. When he went into the chapel, if only for a passing visit, he would stand for a time with his hand on the doorhandle before he entered the presence of his "Master and Lord," as he delighted in calling Jesus.

When we think of this example, and when we think of ourselves, and the way we run unreflectingly into prayer, and when afterwards we complain that we could not pray at all, but that our minds were wandering all the time, perhaps if we cared we could find the cause of these distractions very easily. If, before we began our prayer, we would steady our mind, withdraw it from its surroundings, and turn it in the direction along which we wish it to go, perhaps we should find a growing power of self-control. And this is especially true, and especially necessary, in any such prayer as tries to be independent of forms, such as has been here illustrated.

# SOME HINTS ON PRAYER

## IV

A CORRESPONDENT has suggested a difficulty in his prayer which is well worth our consideration. He opens his prayer-book; he reads, let us say, the prayers before or after Confession; the words are good, he is pleased to have them and to say them; but all the time he has the suspicion that they are not his own. He comes to Confession with the weight of sin upon him; he hopes and believes that by doing what is enjoined upon him he will be freed from his burden; he makes his Act of Contrition, he renews his Purpose of Amendment, with all the earnestness of which his soul is capable; but he tells himself all the time that he has done this kind of thing before, and nothing much has come of it; and he wonders to himself whether all the time he is not soothing himself with mere words, since his resolution seems to come to so little.

In the first place, for his consolation, and for the consolation of the very many who labour under the same suspicion of themselves, let us say at once that this very attitude of mind is in itself a good sign, almost a sure sign, that all is well. In most things in life, and in prayer not least of all, it is not so much what a man can do that is his true measure, but rather what with all his heart he aspires to do; human nature is surrounded with too many obstacles, is weighed down with too many burdens of all kinds, is of itself too weak and faltering, to be a true gauge of the workings of that inner self which, after all, is the true man. We aspire to higher and better things; we make the effort to rise to them; by word and deed we encourage ourselves in our endeavour; in the end we may fail, or may seem to fail, but God has seen our heart, and our effort, as well as our apparent failure, and knows that the evil we do is not the whole story of ourselves.

In the second place this very suspicion is in itself a sure sign of progress. The man who makes an Act of Contrition without any thought whether he means it or not, who learns little of himself from repeated falls and infidelities, who trusts himself this time, as he has often done before, without much intention of greater effort, is in a far more evil plight than the man who knows his weakness, and who can do little more than look up to heaven and cry: "Lord, be merciful to me, a sinner!" —Yes, even though while he cries he trembles for himself in the future.

For a perfect Act of Contrition the main

point is to be utterly sincere, or as sincere as we can make ourselves, at the moment that we pray; this sincerity, forcing our heart to correspond with our words, is the chief object at which we have aimed in these instructions. It may be well, then, to analyse an Act of Contrition in this light, in order both that we may the more clearly discover our own sincerity, and that we may be the more thorough in our contrition in the future.

For practical purposes it may be said that an Act of Contrition consists of three parts, each of which is really a test of the sincerity of the other two. It contains (1) an acknowledgment that I have done wrong, (2) an expression of regret that I have done it, (3) a determination that, because it is wrong, I will not do it again. That contrition may be supernatural each of these must be referred in some way to God; hence they must be rewritten in some such words as the following: (1) an acknowledgment that I have offended God, (2) an expression of sorrow that I have offended Him, (3) a determination that, because this deed is an offence to Him, it shall not be done again. It is a question of the moment when the Act of Contrition is made, not of the past or the future; I may have fallen often in the past, I may fall again in the future, but if here and now my contrition includes, sincerely, each of the three parts just mentioned, then it is true, and, what is more, in the long run it will have its effect.

As has just been said, each of these is a test and proof of the sincerity of the rest. Do I really acknowledge that what I have done is wrong? Then I shall be sorry for having done it; if I am not sorry, it is a sign I am not quite sincere in my acknowledgment. Am I really sorry for what I have done? Then not only shall I wish I had not done it, but I shall determine that, so far as I am able, it shall not occur again. Am I really determined it shall not occur again? Then I will go back to the beginning, look and see where the wrong came in, and take means that in the future it shall be eliminated; in other words I shall determine to avoid, not only sin, but also its occasions. In this last lies the real test of our sincerity; if the determination does not reach as far as the occasions of sin, it is a sign we are not whole-hearted in our condemnation of it, and therefore our contrition is not perfect.

That we may be the more sure of sincerity in our contrition, it will be found by experience that the deeper our motive the more true will contrition be. Fear, for instance, will make us repent in some measure, but it will not touch the heart of the matter; that is why we speak of sorrow built on fear as imperfect contrition. Sorrow founded on a sense of duty is better; founded on devotion it is better still; it is best of all when it is founded on the realisation of offended love. This is why so much depends on our attitude to God when we make our Act of Contrition; if we look upon Him as merely our Judge our contrition is of one kind, if as our lawful Master it is of another, if as our Leader it is yet a third; but it is best of all when we look upon Him as Love offended by what we have done—Love in Himself, Love in Friendship with ourselves, Love atoning for our deeds by enduring every stab they inflict.

It may now be best to give some kind of Act of Contrition, not merely which shall be an act, but which shall help to secure the sinner's sincerity. I have the burden of my sin upon my conscience; I would gladly be rid of that burden; I know that God can free me from it; I know He will free me if I am sincerely sorry for my offence against Him. So I come before Him; I recall to myself Who He is, and who I am in comparison; I let my thoughts and affections then run on, repeating each that I may be sure that I mean them.

### An Act of Contrition

My God,
My Creator,
My Master,
My Friend and Lover,
My Judge,

Almighty yet all-merciful,
All angry yet all-loving,
All just yet all-seeing,
This evil thing I have done,
Evil in itself,
Evil in its degrading consequences,
Evil in its offensiveness to you,
For you have forbidden it,
You detest it,
It violates your law, your order,
It in some way hurts you,
I have done this thing,
I deserve the consequences,
I have no excuse,
Father, forgive me.
I have offended you,
The creature the Creator,
The slave the Master,
The beloved the Lover,
The culprit the Judge,
I deserve the consequences,
I have no excuse,
Father, forgive me.
I have offended you,
The son the Father,
The brother the Brother,
I have crucified your Son, Jesus,
I deserve the consequences,
I have no excuse,
Father, forgive me.
I wish I had not done it,

For my own sake,
For the sake of others,
But most for your sake,
For the sake of Jesus Christ,
I have hurt Him,
Hurt Him in His tender heart,
It shall not happen again,
With your help it shall not,
Though my evil nature craves,
Though my weakness fears,
I am determined,
For my own sake,
For your sake more than mine,
I will take the means,
To keep it far from me,
To avoid the danger,
To put it out of my life,
And all that leads to it,
But I am needy and poor,
O God! help me.

Concluding with the "Our Father," the "Our Father" itself becomes an act of perfect contrition.

# PIETY AND PIETISM

IT is sometimes said, perhaps more often it is felt, that pious people are a dreadful bore. They were "all right" until they became pious; now they are utterly unbearable. Once we could talk to them, could join them in work or in play; now they will not talk, or if they do, the talk turns into piety that makes us stamp with rage; they will not play, or if they do, they make us feel that it is all "out of charity" to us; we cannot even work alongside of them any more than we can work alongside of an iceberg, or while rolling on a bed of thistles.

Nay more, and this troubles us most of all, nothing seems to make us ourselves so impious as contact with these pious people. In their absence we were "all right" and are "all right"; the moment they come into the room, our bristles instantly rise, our tongues become sharpened, our hearts are bitter as gall, our thoughts become unconquerable, so great is the storm that stirs them. When they are gone, it is well if we do not pursue them, or blacken the room they have left, with a torrent of abuse and contradiction that will give us endless remorse, and yet will be defended by us as just, and necessary, and deserved.

There are few who have not undergone this remarkable experience; let us own up to it and acknowledge that there are few who do not undergo it still. Yet surely the experience is remarkable; if philosophy, of every school but one, is correct, then goodness should attract, not repel, and a good man, a holy man, a pious man, should be always a treasure. How, then, are we to account for this apparent contradiction? Goodness is always attractive in theory; in practice, goodness, when it once takes hold of a man, seems to make him simply repelling.

In the first place let us be prepared to give and take; I mean, let us be prepared to own that there may be fault on both sides. The "good" man may be the intolerable bore that we think him, but it may also be that we ourselves are not wholly without blame. I once knew a man whom I thought pious and who occasionally got on my nerves; one day I discovered that he too actually thought me pious, and that accounted for much. He was trying to live up to what he thought my level, and I was giving him a very bad lead.

Or again there may be another cause. We are told that "Birds of a feather flock together;" we are also told that "Two of a trade cannot agree." Whatever be the truth of the first of these proverbs—proverbs are never more than partial truths—it is abundantly true that too much understanding, too great intimacy, tends to make us very critical. He is a great saint indeed who, on close acquaintance, does not give some matter for complaint; and the holier one may be in some respects, the more do we exact from him in others. If "no man is a hero to his valet," neither is any man a saint to his brother; for either the brother knows too much, or else his standard utterly excludes all defect.

There is yet another possibility, which may mean a fault on our side. After all, a good man among us is usually to us a constant admonition. We are holding a certain conversation; our "pious" friend comes in and instinctively we have to stop; he is a nuisance to us—but why? We are having a jolly time, reckless of consequences, perhaps a little reckless of duty; our "pious" friend is seen on the offing; we shirk his company—but why? We are arguing ourselves into a course of action that our conscience all the time disavows; we consult our "pious" friend, and instead of seeing as we see he takes the side of conscience; such a friend is a wet blanket, a croaking pessimist, a soured misanthrope, an unsympathetic creature who will see no point of view but his own; but why this torrent of abuse? Is the fault his or ours?

These then are some of the lines along which, when we condemn, we may not be wholly without blame. We may be opposed to good just because it is good; and since this is against human nature, human nature invents another good which it sets itself up to defend. No saint was ever yet oppressed, but it was shown that he was the enemy of good; no martyr was ever put to death but for apparently the best of causes; and among ourselves no good man is ever hardly judged but the soundest reasons can be given. Nevertheless it may very well be that the saint, and the martyr, and even the good man have right on their side after all.

But even when all this is said, even when we have acknowledged our own possible mistakes and delinquencies, it still remains true that in very many cases, and without any reason like those above mentioned, the "pious" man is a horrid nuisance. Before his retreat he was natural, now he is as stiff, and artificial, and unbending, as only a retreat can make him. Before he was considerate and forgiving, now he is critical and exacting, as though he had no faults of his own. Before he kept what piety he possessed to himself; now he must for ever be improving the occasion, even such as need not be improved. Worst of all, for it is the very worst, before he did not matter much either way; now his very presence makes us bristle, his very silence makes us noisy, even in our prayers, in church or chapel, the mere consciousness that he is beside us banishes what spiritual feelings we may have cherished.

This is undoubtedly true. Undoubtedly there are pious people who do get upon our nerves, even when piety alone is considered. But let us see who they are. To begin with, there are the beginners; not all, but some are a trial, even as are most beginners of almost every kind. If they are true beginners they are sure to be enthusiastic; and the enthusiastic, to those who are not, are always something of a trial. Again, if they are beginners, they are bound to be awkward; they are bound to over-do their part; they are bound to make mistakes; in all this they are something of a trouble. Beginners, again, either ask too many questions from their eagerness to learn or else, because of their inexperience, are liable to make sweeping statements; in all this they can offend.

But these are not half so bad as those who are older. There are some pious people on whom piety acts like starch. They would seem to have taken their models from stained glass windows, not from the saints they represent. Their ideal of spotlessness is a white marble statue, not a red human heart. Their method of devotion is ready-made, turned out

by machinery; it is not made to each individual's measure. Their dealings with others
are puritanical; it begins by looking for flaws,
it condemns whenever it can, it yields to no
one's weakness, it judges all by standards of
its own. These are the people who try us;
the "unco guid," as the genial poet has called
them, or else the "unco dense" who cannot
see other points of view than one.

I do not know whether in our hearts there
are any other pious people we blame. At first
we incline to blame all, sweeping all into one
condemnation. Later we discover that not
all are included; some good people are also
good sorts. Gradually, if we are patient, we
limit very much our sentence; we begin to discover that it is not so much piety we condemn,
or so much piety that rouses us, as either piety
eccentric, or else piety gone mad, or lastly
piety that has frozen into pietism. Man is too
true to be easily mistaken; truth recognises
truth and always loves it; if then there is
antagonism there will be untruth on one side
or the other. But if piety is genuine, if it
goes deep down and is therefore spontaneous,
then it is always welcome; and that chiefly
because it is scarcely, if at all, recognised. It
is blended with the character of the owner,
and the character, chastened by it, dominates.
Such a character we call real, and are prepared
to accept all the rest.

All this leads us to two conclusions. In the first place let us not be in too great a hurry to condemn all piety as pietism. If we have a natural prejudice against piety, and cannot account for its origin, if we have here and there met a pious individual who has got very much on our nerves, let us not hastily assume that all piety is annoying, that all good people are wet blankets, but let us look around and count the number of those whom we revere, not in spite of, but because of their piety.

And secondly let us look to ourselves. It may be that pious people are a trouble to us, chiefly because our piety is a trouble to them. We ourselves may not be immaculate in that matter. Or again it may be that they trouble us, because we do not want to be troubled. We have settled down in a comfortable little puddle of our own, and object to being disturbed. In either case the fault may be ours; if it is, do not let piety suffer for it, even if we ourselves do not aspire so high.

# LIVING IN THE PRESENT

Our Lord said, at the conclusion of the Sermon on the Mount: "Sufficient for the day is the evil thereof;" and He went on to explain the practical application of His words: " Be not therefore solicitous for to-morrow; for the morrow will be solicitous for itself." By this He does not encourage carelessness, or want of foresight; He does not condemn thrift and prudence; He only warns us against the commonest source of all our vainest anxieties, the imaginary fear of what may be. Of all the many kindnesses of God to man, is there any kindness greater than the permission to live each day as a life apart, to make of each day a perfect thing, unspoiled by what may have been, still more by what may be? And yet is there any kindness of God more commonly neglected, more recklessly thrown away?

We human beings are strange creatures. We are for ever crying for the moon, and neglect the solid earth on which we stand. We make nothing of that which is in our hands; our eyes are for ever wandering abroad, seeing phantoms through the mist, turning life into a nightmare, paralysing action by the fear of that which is not. We have the present

always with us; yet we are always endeavour-
ing to live in a half-forgotten past or a fancied
future. We live in the past, recalling pleasures
that are no more, magnifying them out of all
proportion, contrasting with them in their
magnified state the trifling pleasures of to-day,
and by the contrast robbing these pleasures of
their meaning. Or again we look along the
past, and count up the mistakes we have made.
We tell ourselves of all the opportunities we
have lost; our old self scolds our juvenile self
for all the foolish things it has done; we weep
over all that is past and gone; even when we
smile at happy recollections it is with the smile
that lingers round the mouth of a corpse. And
the result of each and all is the same. We
look at the present with a long and sour face.
We say we have spoiled ourselves, or that our
chance is over and will not return, or that
evidently we are doomed to disappointment;
and beneath this self-accumulated burden we
just sit down and do nothing.

Or else we live in the future. We are something at present, but it is nothing in comparison with what we may yet hope to be; we can
do something to-day, but compared with what
we might do, or yet may do, or but for this or
that interference would do, it is not worth
consideration. We peer into the darkness to
discover that which we can never know. We
imagine strange things which we know very

well may never come to pass. We look down imaginary vistas, build our castles in the air, and fret because we are not permitted to live in them. Or last of all, as a last perversion, if for the moment all is going well with us, we deliberately spoil the content we might enjoy by dwelling on the time when we shall be no longer happy, or even, if we are extreme, by making ourselves miserable because we are not so.

Obviously in neither of these ways do we benefit ourselves or others, or promote our good or happiness; by both we only wreck ourselves in the present, so far as we are able. Looking backward has many dangers. In the first place we easily magnify the things that are gone. We forget that in the past we were younger; and the younger we were, the greater do small things appear. Who has not experienced that sense of disappointment which often comes to one who returns to a spot after a long lapse of years? In his childhood he has been in some room or building; he has retained the memory of his visit; in his manhood he visits the spot again, and is oppressed with a sense of its narrowness, its puny size. So it is with much that is past. We retain the recollection, but we forget that we have grown; if time could go backwards, and put us again in the circumstances after which we hanker, how narrow they would seem! how great would be our disappointment!

If this is true of past delights how much more is it true of past miseries! Of all delusions perhaps none is so great as the thought that our past has ruined our present, that the evils we have done, the mistakes we have committed, have made all further hope impossible. Again, for the most part, looking into the past we repeat the mistake of the magnified room. "When I was a child," says St. Paul, "I spoke as a child, I understood as a child, I thought as a child. But when I became a man, I put away the things of a child." So we, when we were children, may indeed have done evil as children; but let us remember it was "as children," and not as mature men and women. And so of every step after; we are always older than we were, always more mature than we were, and the resolve now, if only we will make it, is the act of a more matured creature than the evil we did yesterday. No matter who we are, if we will, it is always in our power to restore the balance.

In the same way dreaming of the future, of what might be and what may be, has at least three paralysing effects. It requires no great imagination to picture to ourselves some state or condition better than that which is now ours. If only this obstacle were removed, if that arrangement were made, if we ourselves were placed in such or such surroundings, how happy we should be! How much good we should be able to do! And we compare our lot with this mirage of our own making; we lose sight of the opportunities that are actually around us; we forget how much worse is the lot of many others; we ignore how little we deserve even of that which is ours; we are depressed at what we have not, neglecting that which we have; our strength is enfeebled, our activity grows slack; we have chosen to live in dreamland, and we reap a dreamer's harvest.

Or there is the other side, the dwelling on imaginary fears. If we are inclined to magnify the pleasures that are past, no less do we magnify the troubles that may be before us. It is a common saying that pain in prospect is greater pain than pain which actually is upon us; or to put it in another way, it is not so much pain, as the prospect of its long continuance that will break a man down. So it is in most things else. If only this will not happen, we shall be happy and content! We have no reason to suppose that it will; but we must worry ourselves with this shadow. If we lose this friend we lose everything; if we lose this situation we are doomed; if this thing goes wrong the rest is hopeless; with these and a thousand other "ifs" we shatter our moral nerve, we take the heart out of our life's work, and render ourselves very puny things indeed.

Meanwhile the present alone is ours, and we are letting it slip through our fingers. The past is gone, whether for evil or for good, to be stored up in better hands than ours. The future still belongs to God alone; and it is not the least of His wonderful mercies that He keeps it entirely to Himself. It is what I am now, not what I have been or shall be; what I do now, not what I have done or shall do; that here and now matters most, to me, and to God, and to all the world besides. Those who face that which is actually before them, unburdened by the past, undistracted by the future, these are they who live, who make the best use of their lives; these are those who have found the secret of contentment. For such there is no day but it can be lived through, no matter what it may bring; there is no circumstance but it can be put to the best advantage, no matter how contrary and galling. "Now is the acceptable time, now is the day of salvation," cried out St. Paul; and he pushed on from day to day, saying every morning with the Psalmist: "Now I have begun," until he discovered that his many beginnings had enabled him to fight the good fight and to complete his course. To be ready for each day's duty as it comes, that will make us ready, when it comes, for the duty of the last day of all.

# TROUBLE

It is easy to read what St. Teresa is said to have written: "Let nothing trouble thee, let nothing annoy thee; all things pass away." It is easy for those who are at peace themselves to preach to others the importance of not suffering themselves to be troubled. Even to ourselves, in our moments of consolation, or in our times of courage and resolution, it is easy to make up our minds that from this hour we will not let ourselves be troubled any more. Trouble is so opposed, peace of mind is so inculcated by all spiritual writers, that we almost come to think that there is something wrong in being troubled; and often enough, perhaps always, some of us actually measure our spiritual state by the degree of peace or of trouble that reigns within our souls.

This may be very well as a gauge to a certain extent, and with a certain class of people; but for many, perhaps for the great majority, it contains a great fallacy. Without any doubt it is a life time of trouble—I mean internal trouble, and not merely external difficulties—that has been the salvation and perfection of

many. For some it may even be said that the
endurance of trouble, the groping through
black darkness, the endurance of irritation, the
feeling about anxiously in the midst of confusion, and doubt, and temptation, the depression that comes of the inner sense of failure
in things whether spiritual or temporal—the
endurance of trouble in these or other shapes
is a characteristic feature of sanctity.

We can go even further. Twice at least is
it expressly told us of Our Lady that she was
troubled, and on other occasions it is more
than implied; indeed one may say that her
whole life seems scarcely intelligible unless
one assumes a certain jarring element of
trouble running through it all. Of her Son,
Our Lord Jesus Christ, it is still more emphatically true. Five times at least we find Him
described to us as distinctly troubled; not
merely feeling things—for that kind of trouble
was seldom absent from Him—and not merely
enduring annoyance—which, as He said, was
His accepted lot—but emphatically, as we
should say, disturbed in mind because of something that had happened. In trouble, then, as
in everything else, these two have " given us
an example," have come right down to our
level. Can we from their troubles discover
anything for ourselves? Can we draw any
conclusion that will guide us in the troubles
that come upon us; especially as to those

which we might learn to keep under, and those
which, even though they crush us, are still
consistent with sanctity?

Let us take first the troubles of Our Lord.
There is the trouble that came on Him as He
stood over the tomb of Lazarus. "Jesus
therefore," says St. John, the Evangelist, *par
excellence*, of the troubles of Our Lord, "when
he saw her (Mary) weeping, and the Jews that
were come with her weeping, groaned in the
spirit, and troubled himself" (John xi. 33).
He is troubled at the trouble of those around
Him; His sympathy for them makes Him
"groan in the spirit." He is troubled at the
loss of a friend, even though He knows that
He is going to bring him back to life. Even
so, in a memorable sermon, do we see the
sweet soul of St. Bernard break down and
sob at the loss of a friend; and when again he
finds his words, he is unable to continue his
discourse, but must needs proclaim the praises
of the friend he has lost.

Next He is troubled in the midst of the pro-
cession on Palm Sunday. "And when he drew
near," says St. Luke, "seeing the city, he wept
over it" (Luke xix. 41); and the reason immediately follows. He is troubled because He
has been rejected; not on His own account—
He is not indignant, He is not offended, He
says nothing of insult or honour—but because
of the woes that He sees will come to those

who will receive Him not.  So is a priest or a teacher often troubled when he sees a soul deliberately walking to its doom.  So are a father and a mother sometimes troubled because a wayward son or daughter will have his or her way, and will pay no heed to those who know better.  Such trouble, such heart-eating trouble, is consistent with the highest sanctity.

The third occasion is that on which Our Lord describes Himself as troubled, and is one full of mystery.  Some Gentiles had come up to the festival.  They asked that they might be introduced to Him.  An Apostle spoke for them, and He answered with a few words in the middle of which these occur : " Now is my soul troubled.  And what shall I say : Father, save me from this hour.  But for this cause I came into this hour.  Father, glorify my name."  What, here, can the cause of His trouble be?  Is it not that which everyone must feel who sees the number of those who have not yet known the name of God and His Christ?  So was St. Paul continually troubled ; so St. Francis Xavier in the midst of the Eastern heathen ; so the many saints who have burnt with zeal for the house of God, and have spent themselves on its account.

Again, early in the course of the Last Supper He is troubled.  After He had washed the feet of His disciples, and had spoken of the example He had given, St. John says of Him: "When Jesus had said these things he was troubled in spirit: and he testified and said: Amen, amen, I say to you, one of you shall betray me" (John xiii. 21). Surely a legitimate trouble is this, whether we consider the treachery of the friend, or the consequences to the traitor. And let us not make too much of the second of these alternatives; that the first ate into the soul of Our Lord is clearly evidenced from the words of Our Lord spoken to the traitor in the Garden: "Friend, whereto art thou come?—Judas, dost *thou* betray the Son of Man?" Treachery must always give trouble, even though we may have the courage at the same time to "rejoice that we are accounted worthy to suffer for the name of Christ"; but the treachery of a friend is the cruellest of all.

Lastly, there is the hour of greatest trouble, that which preceded and culminated in the Agony in the Garden. The Evangelists vie with each other in looking for words by which to express it. "He began to be sorrowful and to be sad," says one. "He began to fear and to be heavy," says another. "Being in an agony, he prayed the longer," says the third; and all record His words: "My soul is sorrowful even unto death." Nor do even these English words convey the full sense of amazement and depression that is contained in the

Greek original. He is so troubled that He seems to be unable to help Himself; He seeks support from others—from His disciples, and they fail Him, from His Father, and at first it seems to be long in coming, from an angel, who does not remove the trouble, but brings Him the support He needs. And why is He so troubled? Because of "the chalice," whatever that may mean. We cannot hope to know all; but we can draw out some few ingredients. He was troubled because He had been, and yet would be, rejected. He was troubled because He loved so much those who had rejected Him. Perhaps most of all He was weighed down by the burden of their sins, which He had taken upon Himself as though they were His own.

So has the burden of the evil-doing of mankind oppressed the hearts and souls of men who have recognised it—the popes in all ages, the saints whose lot it has been to rule, the weary priest in our crowded cities, all we may say who have been given the care of others. Of all the troubles of man perhaps none more conduces to indignation; perhaps there is none which tempts us more to steel our hearts, and to leave man to his self-inflicted doom. Yet when the temptation is upon us it is well to remember that just this trouble, harrowing as it is, death-dealing to our own spiritual peace of mind as it is, nevertheless brings us nearer to Our Lord in his worst moments than does any other prayer or sacrifice.

Now let us put alongside of these the two expressed troubles of Our Lady. First is that which she felt at the Annunciation. When the angel had come in, and had saluted her with his greeting: "Hail, full of grace, the Lord is with thee, blessed art thou among women;" the Evangelist adds that Mary " having heard was troubled at his saying, and thought within herself what manner of salutation this should be." She was troubled, but not in doubt, as was Zachary on a like occasion. She was troubled because, as is said of her several times afterwards, " she did not understand." There was something new, something of a revolution in all this; she did not know to what it pointed; the will of God for her had become confused. So have the greatest saints been troubled at moments of crisis in their lives. So for example was St. Teresa often troubled. So is many a soul troubled that seeks earnestly to find that will, and is suffered to remain in the dark.

The next occasion is far more easily understood. She had lost her Son; she had looked for Him three long days; when she found Him the trouble of her heart would not contain itself. "Son, why hast thou done so to us?" she said. "Behold thy father and I have sought thee sorrowing." This is a trouble

that needs no explanation, and needs no
parallel. Whatever commentators may say as
to the possible self-accusation in Our Lady's
heart, the simple fact is quite enough; she
had lost Him—she, Him—and he is a strange
nature who does not understand the rest. But
perhaps there are some who understand it
more than others; not merely good mothers
who have been forced to part with a child they
have loved, but those who at some time in
their lives have been permitted to draw very
near to their Lord, and then afterwards have
seemed to lose Him. How many of this kind
have cried: "Why hast thou done so to us?"
and have been told that it was because of "His
Father's business"! Let such remember the
troubled heart of Our Lady.

We are not told of other troubles of hers,
even at times when it might have been expected. We are not told that she was troubled
at the birth of her Child in poverty and want,
or at the painful prophecy of Simeon, or
because they were cruelly driven into exile, or
when she wished to see her Son and, apparently, could not see Him, or even when she
stood beneath His cross and watched Him
bleed slowly to death. That there was trouble
we know; but we are not told of it. All we
see is the quiet, enduring Mother, "keeping
these things, and pondering them in her
heart"; the model of many a silent, suffering

woman, who sees, and feels, and says nothing while her heart within her is breaking. Here, then, again we have an aspect of trouble which many of us can appreciate.

From these examples, then, we can safely conclude that a troubled heart is not always a heart that is faltering or faithless. There are troubles from without and troubles from within which are consistent with perfection; to kill the power of feeling these troubles, to put ourselves in this sense beyond the reach of trouble, may be very good philosophy—let philosophers look to that!—but it is no special imitation of Our Lord and His Mother. To be troubled at the loss of a friend is possible for a saint; to be above such trouble means, if anything, something on the other side. It is good to be troubled when the will of God is not done among men. It is good to be troubled at the failure of those who are clearly called to high emprises. It is consistent to be troubled when God leaves us, as He does at times, wholly in the dark; in these and many other ways may trouble come to a faithful soul.

But there are many other troubles which we can well afford to lay aside. What are they? Their number is legion; and we shall know what they are as they come to us, if only we will cling to Him who is the Prince of Peace. It was of these that He spoke when he said:

"Let not your heart be troubled, nor let it be afraid. You believe in God, believe also in me." And it was to those who were troubled in this way that He cried: "Come to me, all you that labour and are burdened, and I will refresh you. Take up my yoke upon you, and learn of me, because I am meek and humble of heart: and you shall find rest to your souls. For my yoke is sweet and my burden light."

Our Lord was troubled in the Garden, but we are not told that He was troubled at the sight of the Cross.

# FRIENDSHIP

WHAT do I mean by a friend? I mean something that is almost too much to be looked for in this world. I mean one whose nature is so large that it will understand and sympathise with all my myriad varied moods. I mean a man who, when he finds me mean and grovelling, will not despise me; when he sees me harsh and critical, will not condemn my hardness of heart; when I am cruel in judgment, or in word, or in action, will bear with me till I recover my senses; when I am proud, or vain, high-handed, or inflated with myself, will smile and endure knowing that this is only a passing whim; when I am ill-tempered, or peevish, or melancholy, will pity me and wait till the disease has run its course, and the colour of health has returned.

I mean by a friend one who will give as well as take. I mean one who, when he in turn is in trouble, will not hide it from me. I mean one who will not give me the everlasting feeling that the weakness is all mine, while he is in possession of unending peace and calm. I mean one who will trust me far enough to let me see his weakness as I let him see mine, knowing that I too will not misunderstand, or misinterpret, or become impatient, or condemn, or turn upon my heel and walk no more with him, even as I know he will not do the like to me. This is the other side of friendship harder to discover than the first; yet if one would be my friend, in the deep sense in which I understand it, he must give me this as I give the same to him; he must trust me thus far, even as I trust him; if he is only my patron, my protector, my guide, my model, my ideal, he may be very much to be loved and honoured, but he is not strictly my friend.

I mean by a friend one with whom there are no differences. Whatever be our respective gifts of nature and of grace, it must be all the same between him and me. If he thinks me clever, or learned, or strong, or even holy, he will neither bow before me, nor treat me as a being of another grade; though I may know him to have rank, or wealth, or athletic skill, or wit, these things, when I think of him, will scarcely enter my mind. We take each other for granted, without suspicion, without reserve, without doubt; the rest are mere appendages, belonging to one as much as to the other, affecting so little our equality that we never give them a thought.

Such is what I mean by a friend; so perfect a union is friendship. But where is such a friend? Am I asking too much of human nature? Is a relation so perfect possible in this life? I wonder. The young soul sets out on its journey, and hopes to find such a comrade on its way. It takes hold of first one and then another, telling itself that it has found what it needs; but how often has it been disappointed! First it gave its friendship to one older than itself, and soon discovered it had a patron, not a friend; good, true, loyal, sound, but not what it meant by a friend. For this first would-be friend, for all the longing soul gave, showed but one side in return; he was too good, too loyal, too sound—let us say it—to be wholly true. He had the strength to guide, the virtue to endure; he lacked the humility which is essential to the ideal of friendship.

This has been the commonest disappointment of my life; that hardening of friendship into mere patronage, that murder of friendship because my friend would not let me see him as he was. I gave him all; he gave me back but my own reflection; himself he hid behind the mirror. I say nothing of false friends or of shallow friends. These are incapable of friendship; and to have found them out, to have fathomed all their possibilities, to have weighed them in the balance and found them wanting, is no disappointment; it is a growth in the knowledge of mankind. Disappointment only comes when one has proved and knows the possibility of friendship, and behold! it has frozen in the making.

And yet there have been satisfactions. There have been moments when, as it were, in spite of itself, friendship has broken through the mist and glimmered golden. An old man, a superior of mine, once, in a moment of great trouble, came for refuge to my room and there burst into tears; that was a moment of happy agony, a moment of perfect friendship. Once, in a crowd of great men and ladies, where I was but a mechanical official, there passed me by a man who had been a schoolfellow, whom I had not seen since school-days, and that was years ago. He saw me, I saw him; not a word passed between us; I have never seen him since; yet that moment was a moment of perfect friendship. More I will not say by way of illustration, lest friendship itself resent this public avowal.

Yes, friendship, even of the kind that is here meant, is possible in its degree, for the nature of man is beyond fathoming, his capabilities of love are only short of infinite. Still it is only in its degree. Even from the best of human friends I must not ask more than he can give. For think of all it calls for. It calls for a mind that can understand mind without any need of words. It calls for a heart that can bleed more from sympathy and fellow-feeling than from any suffering of its own. It

calls for a soul so holy, so humble in its holiness, that it will give of its all, of its worst as
well as of its best, uncovered and undisguised
into the hands of its friend. It calls for a will
that can go all lengths, asking no questions,
making no conditions, when the question of
friendship demands it. "Who is weak and I
am not weak? Who is scandalised, and I am
not on fire?"—"Greater love than this no
man hath, that he lay down his life for his
friend." Where is all this to be found, united
in any one human being? Where indeed!

Insist on the last drop of blood, and you will
find it nowhere; nowhere except in One.
There is no human friendship but it can be
snapped, none but it can be tried beyond its
strength, even though it means the death of
the one or the other. In One only is it
invincible. One mind alone understands,
better far than I understand myself, and has
understood from the beginning, without any
need of words of mine to tell it. One heart
has bled, first from Its own crushing, but more
because of the crushing of my heart, and
bleeds on still, the more when my own has
ceased to do so. One soul has made Itself in
all things like to mine, has shown me all It has
and all It is, Its strength and Its seeming
weakness, Its gladness and Its broken part,
Its temptations, Its indignations, Its tears, Its
appeals for help, Its cries of pain, and distress,

and desolation. One will alone has refused to set limits alike to Its giving and to Its receiving, has asked for no terms, has made no stipulations, has found me as I am, and has become one with me, my good and my evil, my weakness and my strength, without a word, without a thought of what It set aside for my sake. One alone has not only borne my sorrows and carried my griefs, but has shown me His own, has "become sin" for me, has made Himself one with me and taken all the consequences; and yet withal, remains unexhausted. There is still no cry that He has given enough, that He can descend no lower, that He declines to show me, even me, every side of His nature.

Then have I not reason to be contented? I show Him all my failures and my troubles, knowing that He does not merely listen, and pity, and patronise, but gives me of His own, and lets me see His wounds and His weakness in return. I bring Him all my strength, my little doughty deeds of which I am so childishly proud, and I know He does not make too much of my vainglory, much less does He make too much of me. Instead, He rejoices with me when I rejoice, weeps with me when I weep, but then, and most of all, swallows up my rejoicing and weeping in His own. Yes, even on earth, I have found a perfect friend. *Inveni quem diligit anima mea, tenui eum nec dimittam*—" I have found Him whom my soul loveth; I have held Him and will not let Him go." *Illum dilige, et amicum tibi retine, qui, omnibus recedentibus, te non relinquet, nec patietur in fine perire. Ab omnibus oportet te aliquando separari, sive velis, sive nolis*—" From all others, willy nilly, you must some day be torn apart. Love Him and keep Him for your friend, Who, when all else secedes, will not leave you, nor suffer you to perish in the end!" (*Imit. Xti.* ii. 7).

# ONE ANOTHER

IT does not require much insight or philosophy
to discover that in spite of much that appears
on the surface, and in spite of endless warnings and gruesome pictures, human nature is
not wholly evil. Nay more, we can without
much fear go further and say that no human
being was yet made who was wholly evil.
Shakespeare tried to create one; but he
acknowledged in the end that the being he
had created was not human. Dickens tried
several times over; but he did so only by omit-
ting the human element in every case; the
more fiendish are his characters, the less are
they drawn from life. In some human beings,
it is true, the good that is in them may be
much covered over; in others it may have had
little opportunity for development; in others,
again, it may be of a nature so little akin to
the good that is in ourselves that we almost
call it something else; yet others may have so
preponderating a balance of evil in their com-
position that the good may be utterly eclipsed.

None the less is it there somewhere. Human
nature being what it is, we cannot doubt that
it is never wholly evil; that belongs to the
devil only, and even of the devil there are

points of view which leave us mystified. At all events I do not know a description of a devil in literature which does not leave one with some sense of sympathy. Milton's devils are admirable; Dante's devils stir our pity; Goethe's devil makes us feel what a good thing has been wasted. Human nature seems incapable of imagining that which is wholly bad, just because it is not wholly bad itself.

It follows from this that a man can, if he likes, always have a kindly feeling for his fellow-man, no matter what may be the provocation to the contrary. Indeed he has a duty to do so; and the greater he is, the less will he be influenced by a single point of view, the more will he endeavour to see all round, and upon the whole conception to pass his judgment. Let us then, in our dealings with others, remind ourselves of one or two principles, quite platitudinous in themselves, but which, nevertheless, if we will keep them in mind, will save us many a rash judgment, and harsh word, and hasty action. For such things are the characteristics of small people; when we ourselves are guilty of them, we know how puny and despicable we are in our own eyes, and in those of others; moreover they cultivate puniness, and react upon their perpetrators in a multitude of ways.

The first principle is to accept what has already been said, that is, to believe in everybody; let us call it the principle of faith. There are some who preach the opposite; they say the prudent man will believe in nobody. But the doctrine of such people condemns itself; for it forbids us to believe in them. If they merely said: "Put implicit faith in nobody," they might have a case; for there is no one who has not a weak point somewhere, on which, for his sake as well as for our own, it is unfair to put too much reliance. But there is a world of difference between putting an implicit trust in others and believing in them. The former may be, and more often than not is, an act of weakness, a mere leaning for self-support, an endeavour to shift one's own responsibility to the shoulders of another; the latter is the deliberate act of a strong man, and is usually a support and strengthening to others even more than to oneself. By believing in others, then, we mean the conviction that the evil a bad man may do does not represent the whole man; that the failure of a man does not show all his capabilities; that whatever may be a man's weakness, it is usually only a covering for something very strong and beautiful underneath. We may pass by unnoticed a quiet, harmless, passive creature, and ignore him with the pitying comment that he has nothing in him; but we may also be ignoring as deep a soul as we shall ever meet in our lifetime. We may set aside a man because he is a miserable failure; but we may be also trampling on a throbbing, bleeding heart, whose yearnings are far greater than our own, which feels its failures greater than do we, which has failed while we have succeeded chiefly because its ideals are greater than ours.

Or again, we may be roused to indignation against some confirmed criminal, some utterly bad man. But we may not know that the same poor creature is equally disgusted and indignant with himself; that it is his circumstances more than himself that stand responsible for his condition; that if we had had his chances and no more, our fate would have been a poor thing; that even as it is his outlook is such as would make us happier creatures envious; that for all his wickedness there are nevertheless those who know him better than we, and understand him better than we, and have an unaccountable attraction and affection for something he possesses. Even Bill Sykes was loved by Nancy—and by his dog; and to be loved with sincerity by one who knows us implies something in us that is lovable. Who that has dealt much with criminals has not felt this lovableness peering out in all sorts of places?

The second principle is that of hope; and this means that we should be confident that no good deed we ever do is wasted. It is true we may fail in our immediate object; we may not always gain the good effect we intended. We may work for a conversion, and our friend may die without any sign of having once ever given the matter a thought. We may give an alms and find we have only been encouraging a wastrel. We may labour to exhaustion in teaching a child, and the child may turn out nothing but a shame to its instructors. Still none of these cover the whole matter. A good deed done is like a stone dropped in deep water; the circles of waves continue to go out from that centre, on and on, and to and fro, long after the stone has settled at the bottom.

Let us examine these cases in some detail. I teach a child and seem to myself to have failed, to have wasted my time and energy. But others do not see it in the same light; the child itself does not. Others have been stimulated by that which I have done, in ways and to efforts altogether out of my ken. The child itself has a memory stored away in its heart, which some day will lead to its repentance. And besides these waves of blessing that have been started, with results more far-reaching than any dream of mine would have fancied, there is the lasting good done to myself, there is the fulfilment of a noble duty to mankind, there is the glory of a sacrifice given to God, there is the likeness to Jesus Christ, then most of all when my effort is least rewarded; and

none of these may be neglected in the
reckoning.

So again with a wasted alms. I may not
approve of promiscuous alms-giving, but that
does not prevent me from seeing that even
promiscuous alms-giving is not wholly bad.
Nine times out of ten I may be cheated; but if
the tenth time I failed, in a case of real distress, could I ever forgive myself? And
besides it is not every wastrel that is wholly
reprobate; even among tramps there have
been saints. The wastrel who meets you may
not deserve your penny; if he receives it he
may even chuckle at his fortune, and your
weakness; nevertheless, as often as not, he
goes away with something more than a penny
in his hand, something in his heart of which
he is not aware, but which some day will bear
fruit; the memory of one who has treated him
above that which he has deserved, the memory
of a kind deed done. Talk some day, if you
like, with any common tramp. Get his confidence and see what he will have to say; not
with the object of deceiving you, but on a
footing of equality. A hundred to one he
will harp upon one or two subjects; the kindness he has received from someone or other
in a moment of particular crisis, or the wish,
perhaps I should call it despair, lying at the
back of his heart that he could have been or
could be different. He may make no change

in his life after he has spoken; he may show
his deliberate intention to make no change; he
may spend your twopence at the next ale-
house. But he will probably add your memory
to that of others who did not treat him wholly
as a pariah; who for a moment let him feel
that in spite of all he was a man among men.
Perhaps some of us would not think that in
such a case our alms was wholly wasted.

Similarly we might argue about that still
more hopeless matter, the conversion of one
dear to us; more hopeless in one sense, because the special end we have in view seems
so seldom to be gained, but surely not more
hopeless when we think of the supernatural
forces with which we are venturing to deal.
Here more than anywhere else we have the
guarantee of God Himself that our efforts are
not in vain; and in those safe hands we are
content to trust our all.

The third principle is that of charity; which
means that we should take a chance of doing
good when we get it, and should not be too
often on our own defensive. Charity does
not calculate too much, charity is not too dis-
criminating, charity does not care to haggle,
charity does not demand a *quid pro quo*,
charity expects to make many a mistake,
charity shuts its eyes and goes on. This is a
point that needs little development; it only
needs that we should take it to ourselves—pru-

dently and wisely, if we like, but none the less truly and practically. We can always see the beauty of self-sacrificing charity in others; let us not forget that in ourselves it can be no less beautiful. In others we can see its conquering power; the same can it effect in ourselves.

"There remain, then," to use the words of St. Paul, "these three." Faith teaches us to believe in everybody, not as satisfied optimists, but as men amongst our fellow-men. Hope gives us the confidence that nothing we do is wasted. Charity goes further; it bids us not easily to miss a chance of doing good, not to act on the defensive, never to use the argument that we are not obliged as a reason for standing aloof. You want to do something worth doing before you die; seize the opportunities that are given you every day, and in the end you will find that something has been done. Do not be for ever waiting for the great occasion, and fretting because it never seems to come; if you keep waiting, and meanwhile do nothing, either the occasion will never come, or when it comes you will not recognise it, or you will be so utterly unpractised in the art of doing and giving that you will be unable to seize it. On the contrary, make your own occasion; give, and give, and give again. You will find that one great deed will lead to another; your hands will never be empty. There is always work for such workers; this is a profession which is not over-stocked, in which competition is not great, and yet of which the profits are portentous.

Of what kind are those profits? Not always of money, though even in the matter of money it is strange how often genuine charity is re-quited; but rather of blood; not of broad acres, but of human hearts; not perhaps in the goods of this world, where rust and the worm destroy, but in a world where there are no thieves, and canker does not enter.

# THE OTHER SIDE

WHEN we are young we naturally believe in everyone we meet. A child who has had anything like a home has been brought up on trust and confidence; it has not learnt to disbelieve or doubt, at all events those whom it knows. Still, even a child instinctively fears those whom it does not know; a stranger is to it something to be dreaded, something to be suspected of being on the whole more evil than good. When we grow a little older we think we outgrow this fear. But in matter of fact it is commonly more intensified, though it may show itself along another line. Some may call it shyness; some may call it criticism; whatever outward expression it may assume there is a tendency in us to think hard things of those whom we do not know, to picture strangers to ourselves as persons rather to be feared than welcomed, to dread meeting them, and to be anxious even to pain about what we shall find when we make their acquaintance.

Then when the meeting does come, in nine cases out of ten we are agreeably surprised. The stranger is very much like ourselves after all. The great man is not so great; or if he is, he is obviously great against his will. The scholar is a child, the soldier a school-boy magnified; we come across them one by one and condemn ourselves for our preconceived judgments. When we made them we were little better than children; we feared what was unknown; when we come to know it we are ashamed of our fears.

From this it is safe to make a general conclusion, and it is this: Most men are better than the estimate we form of them before we know them. Our first judgments, founded on hearsay, or on some wholly alien evidence, must necessarily be exaggerated; it is deprived of the means of filling in the lights and the shades which personal contact alone can provide. If we hear of another's talents, we magnify the poor victim in our minds till he becomes a perfect monster; if we are told of his strength of will, we imagine some inhuman cyclops; if we have proof of his fascinating personality, we picture some siren of the sea that will lure us, unless we are careful, to our destruction.

Then comes the discovery, and with it often the reaction to the opposite extreme. Monster as the creature of our imagination was, it was nevertheless an idol; we meet the man in real life and find him only human. So that, very often, our second judgments are as unsound as our first. Our monster of intellect falls so short of our anticipation that we declare him to be overrated, forgetting that it is ourselves alone who have done him this injustice. Our strong man never seems to put forth his strength; we wonder whether he really has any. And so with all the rest of the idols which our fancy has set up.

But if this is true of every type of man it is particularly true of those who earn that most unenviable of reputations, the reputation for being good. Poor creatures! What a time such people have! A man is talked about as being holy; he has had the misfortune to utter some spiritual remark, he has been seen to do or not to do something which has been taken as proving his mortified spirit, he has been found somewhere on his knees—perhaps asleep—and the word has gone round that he is a man of prayer. A stranger hears of him and is curious. He wonders whether after all he is going to come across a live saint; whether there will be a halo round his head, whether his hands will have wounds in them, whether his haggard face will bear the marks of long fasting, whether at the very least his eyes will not be for ever closed, or else for ever turned upwards so that the white alone will appear.

Then comes the meeting. There is no halo, perhaps there is instead a rather unruly head of hair. There are no wounds; instead there is a daintiness, almost a foppishness about his fingers that is worthy of a dandy. He has scarcely a wrinkle on his face; on the contrary he is quite aggressively healthy-looking, with not a shade of mortification. His eyes are not cast down, much less are they turned up; rather they twinkle at a joke, look about at every thing of interest, almost make you think of the warning that the eyes are the windows of the soul. And as for his conversation—well, really! He asks how you are; he talks about the weather; he remarks on the news in the morning paper; he discusses some triviality suggested by a book on the table or a picture on the wall; he propounds just the same commonplace platitudes that everybody else drones out. His behaviour is no less disappointing; so uneven, so given to long silence or else to rather inordinate laughter, so easy-going, so ordinary, perhaps even, if we watch him closely, not always in very good taste.

And this is your saint! We forget that it is ourselves who are to blame. We had no business to divorce our ideal from human nature. In our picture we have eliminated a saint's first characteristic, his hiddenness; but besides, and perhaps worse, we have taken the remarks of others and magnified them so that those who uttered them could never have recognised the original. They never said he was a saint; they merely said he was a very human being who suited their fancy. They never said he was mortified; they merely said he did not always take sugar in his tea. They never said he was a man of prayer; they merely found him once fingering his beads. We have added the rest; and the poor man gets a bad time of it at our hands.

When, then, we make up our minds about another, let us give both ourselves and our victim a fair start. The chances are that every man we meet is a human being and not a portent; and every human being has both his weaknesses and his good points. No one is wholly bad, very few are wholly good; if then we hear anyone indiscriminately praised, let us not at once imagine to ourselves an ideal so perfect that we must inevitably be disappointed when we meet. Nor, on the other hand, need we because of our disappointment cancel all that we have heard. Probably the truth lies midway between the two. If the man is not the unrivalled genius we fancied, he may be very talented all the same; if he does not always show his power, it may be there ready for its occasion; if he is not a saint, he may have that in him which makes for sanctity. Few people do not say a good thing sometimes; few are not mortified in some respects; even if there are few who pray, at least there are few who do not desire it, and who do not make the effort sometimes. Or to put our conclusion in another way, if we did not form our judgments of others beforehand we should usually find that our impressions of them would almost invariably be good.

There is another factor which may often warp our estimate of others. The story is told in various forms of the visitor who was being shown through a lunatic asylum by a harmless inmate, sensible on every point but one. As they walked along a corridor they passed another harmless lunatic. "See that man," said the guide, "what do you think is his craze? He actually thinks himself to be the Holy Ghost!" Then, as the visitor made no comment, he added: "Isn't he absurd, considering I am the Holy Ghost myself!"

Now how many of us have a touch of this lunacy in ourselves? How many of us have not noticed that if we fancy ourselves in any way, if we think ourselves rather clever, or strong-willed, or brilliant, or pious, we are inclined to be hard on those who have a reputation for the same. We do not like to own it; we are ashamed of ourselves when we discover it; but there is no more sure proof of vanity than the refusal to brook another star of our particular magnitude in our own horizon. Nor, we may add, is there any more sure proof that we are not that which we imagine ourselves to be. Mere intellectual brilliance resents a rival; a really clever man welcomes the ability of another. Sham strength fears competition; a really strong man rejoices in the strength of a companion. Imitation sanctity must shine alone; a really holy man has no greater satisfaction than the discovery and promotion of another's holiness.

It is often said that the perfection of good manners consists in being perfectly natural and perfectly true. This explains why, in the opinion of very many, the contented poor are often the best-mannered people in the world. Whether the statement be true or not, a very little modification makes it safe. Good manners are founded on a certain give and take. If we are ourselves, neither more nor less, if we take others for what they are, neither less nor more, if we adapt ourselves to them, and them to ourselves, without any presumption or arrogance, then we shall behave as we should. This is the life that is true, in the exterior as well as within; and this is why, when we meet a saint, if we ever do, we shall be most struck, not by his sanctity, nor by his abstraction, but by the yielding deference of his manners. He appreciates the good he finds in others; he shows that good its due respect; and the consequent behaviour is one of those links which inseparably unite the saint with all mankind.

# THE APOSTLE'S GRIEF

" Who is weak, and I am not weak? Who is scandalised, and I am not on fire?"—2 Cor. xi. 29.

THERE are many sufferings in life; I mean, many veins of suffering, along which pain wells from and back to the human heart. But there is one agony distinct from all the rest, which, when felt, gives one a totally new idea of the suffering of the Heart of Christ Our Lord. It is the suffering, the peculiar agonising void, the torture that makes moaning no relief, nor motion of the body any change, which one feels when one watches a soul one dearly loves deliberately exchanging good for evil.

A soul comes across our path; in a very little time we see it to be transparent as crystal, a thing of real beauty, all the more beautiful because it does not know it itself. We revel in the sunshine of its presence, the thought of evil is banished when it is there, at the sight of it, at the thought of it, we thank God that He has made man. Delicate and perfect it has grown up out of and amidst the evil that lies wallowing around it, and by its mere presence there we know that all the rest is worth while.

One day we are puzzled. We can point to nothing in particular, we can lay our hands on nothing; the glittering eye is there, the artless confidence of action is there, even the happy laugh, and frank expression, and merry overflow of words. And yet through and around it all there is something, which we cannot detect, but which was not there before; so thin is the film covering it that we blame ourselves for rash judgment, we tell ourselves that it is at most only a new phase of the soul to which our eyes have not yet been accustomed.

Nevertheless it is there, and remains, and soon finds a clearer definition. The laughing eye still laughs, but perhaps with a certain conscious boldness; the artless confidence of action has something aggressive in it; the frankness is too dramatic, the language too loud, there is an exaggeration somewhere which does not ring true. And once that jarring is discovered, then begin in the chords of one's own heart a sympathetic jarring, a wondering at it knows not what, an aching that will not be located, a wandering of mind, an aimlessness of action, a reaching out to any kind of relief, a yearning to do something where there is nothing to be done, a craving to shed tears which will not come—all these the foresigns of the storm that is about to burst.

Then comes the revelation. It will be in some gesture, some strange accidental word, some attitude of thought expressed in an idle manner which will reveal the terrible truth to the soul that loves. Things are not what they were; the rose has received a canker worm; the word has been uttered, the allusion has been made, the deed has been done, which has opened the understanding eyes of one to whom the poor child is dear, and henceforth it seems that there can be no rest for him again.

No; there is no greater agony in human life than to be compelled to watch a human soul deliberately turning to evil before one's very eyes, above all a soul which has already grown long in innocence. The agony has been too much for many before to-day; it has driven them to murder, or to suicide, or both; they would rather see their child dead but innocent at their feet, than living but beginning to corrupt; they would rather die themselves than live and endure the sight of the robbery of this treasure of their soul. The reckless child laughs at the agony it causes; it refuses to see the harm that is done; it claims its rights; it rests upon its own strength; it turns with indignation against any word of remonstrance; it will do what it likes and no one shall interfere; it knows its own mind and needs no warning; it takes one step cautiously at first, it takes a second more coolly, with the third it gets its stride, the fourth begins to run, and stab, stab, stab, stab, goes down into the heart that loves, and sees, and understands, and knows only too well the inevitable end of that career.

In truth we reckless creatures seldom consider what we are doing when we play fast and loose with right and wrong. We know we make ourselves miserable by it, but we pretend not to care for that; we do not always know how miserable we make others, or if we do we affect not to believe it. But often enough for the sake of someone else we will avoid evil, even when we will not avoid it for our own; and if we would only realise how our own determination hurts the heart of one we love, perhaps we would at least think twice before we acted.

I do not know what good can come of needlessly hurting others; I do not even know what self-satisfaction the most selfish human being can gain by it; yet I do know that many a time in life a soul that is going from good to bad, or from bad to worse, will trample on the hearts of those who love it—a mother's, a father's, a sister's, a brother's, a husband's, a wife's, a truly loving friend's—revelling in the blood that is spilt, even while each stamp of the foot sends agony into its own heart, and when asked why it so acts it will cry out simply that so it chooses. It is the hardest thing to understand in human life, this deliberate defiance of common human feeling by the soul that determines to have its own way; it is the most fruitful cause of misery in every home; yet it is found again and again, and always the cause is the same.

But sometimes there comes an awakening, and then how the tables are turned! The soul that did the harm is embittered for the rest of its life, whether with gnawing remorse, or whether with soothing contrition; it sees what it has done, to itself and to others, it sees what others have done to it and for it, and what they are ever willing to do; and the discovery is terrible indeed. If before there were tears, hard, bitter tears of self-will, now there are tears, many more, from the heart and not only from the eyes.

But they are tears that make others thank God. "Peter, going out, wept bitterly;" but Christ Our Lord rejoiced at the tears that were shed. And so it is often with us. The time may be long, the way may be stony, the agony may drag along, but if we will leave the ninety-nine alone, and go after the strayed one till we find it, please God it will be there at last. And when it is found to be there it is also found to have been worth while—worth all the suffering, the sleeplessness and long-dragging days, though not worth the bitterness of the poor thing that insisted on having its way. "And when he hath found it, doth he not lay it upon his shoulders, rejoicing? And coming home calleth together his friends and neighbours, saying to them: Rejoice with me, because I have found my sheep that was lost? I say to you that even so there shall be joy in heaven upon one sinner that doth penance, more than upon ninety-nine just who need not penance."

# THE SINNER'S GRIEF

IF to look on and watch a beautiful soul deteriorating before our eyes is an agony almost intolerable, if such an agony leaves behind it a scar upon the heart which nothing can ever quite heal, no less is the internal grief of the deteriorating soul itself a thing terrible to witness. In some degree we have all felt it—that grief which conscience inflicts on us when we have done something utterly unworthy; but the deeper, gnawing thing, the grief which turns life into an ocean of bitterness, belongs to the soul which has once been good, which still is good, but which has deliberately accepted some special evil into its nature, and refused to let it go. Such a soul, I do sincerely believe, is the most pitiable thing in all the world; even the great sinner is less in a sense to be pitied, inasmuch as his heart is now hardened and the sense of suffering has been numbed.

Let us watch the process. A child, a youth, a young woman, has learnt by experience what it is to dwell in the tabernacles of the Lord. He has felt the fascination of innocence; he has known what is the happy martyrdom of being fired with the love of Jesus Christ; he has learnt the secret of rejoicing in suffering, or revelling in self-sacrifice, of springing through life with that utter joy of living which belongs peculiarly to the innocent of hand and clean of heart. To such a soul the course is quite clear; it ascends the Mount of God with unhesitating step, the sun of God's own love shines overhead, the way may be long, the stones may be cutting, but the truth of life is manifest, and it has no hesitation, no remorse, no doubts, nothing but the pure delight of giving, and the craving ever to give more.

One day there comes a change, and with a soul like this the method of the change is almost invariably the same. Hitherto it has had no other comrades and companions than the Angels of Light; no others will it consent to know. But one day a new Angel of Light appears upon the way. It may be an Angel from without, in the shape of an external fascination for something apparently good; it may be from within, in the desire to do some good thing, to follow some particular inclination of its own, a conversion of a soul, a special good work, anything which will make it turn aside from the track along which it is drawn.

At first all seemingly goes well. There is fruit to show for one's labour, a soul is drawn towards God by one's attention; and one tells oneself that it is good to sacrifice one's own perfection just a little that another may be profited the more. So this is the next step; one stoops to the soul that is down, one lowers one's own standard a trifle, one gives to the creature one is saving not only its proper due, not only that which, as a creature oneself, one can lawfully bestow upon another, but also a little more, that which belongs irrevocably to one's own best and truest and most loyal Friend.

But the evil does not stop there. No one ever yet did wrong that good might come of it, but sooner or later found reason to repent of his decision. Whether or not the expected good is gained is beside the mark; more often than not we fail to secure what we worked for, but even if we gain it, we have started a new misery that is worse. For to yield to evil is to weaken one's own self, one's soul, one's character, one's power for doing good, one's interior peace of mind; without God no man can do anything, it is only in Him who strengthens us that we can do anything at all. Hence the one evil thing we do leads inevitably to another; we would yield "just this once, and just this far," and we find we have taken the first step in a series of yieldings. We are not what we were; that is the first agony which torrents of tears seem unable to assuage. We are at the mercy of new forces which before had no hold upon us, and we are less able to resist them; that is a second agony which is close akin to despair. We have taken our own course, we have separated ourselves from those who before had held us up; and now, in the darkness and gloom, we are hedged about by a sense of loneliness, and untruth, and helpless weakness, which makes life itself an intolerable burden.

Then comes the struggle. Humility bids us turn back while yet there is time, and, since we cannot help ourselves, take hold of a hand that will help us; but pride whispers in our ear that this will not do, that we are our own masters and must brook no interference, that we have chosen our own path and must needs walk along it to the bitter end. Our lives are now broken, we tell ourselves, we have lost our treasure for ever, and we must carry our grief in our own hearts and work out our doom as best we may.

So is the agony increased at every step, until at last the poor soul becomes partly numbed, tells itself that it has grown used to it, or soon will grow used to it, and meanwhile must submit to the inevitable. It knows it is deceiving itself; it knows the sin—if it is sin—and the agony could be removed by one bold step backward, by one humble trusting of itself to a hand that can and will support it; but these things to human nature are very hard.

Yes, they are very hard; but, thank God, not too hard. "God tempers the wind to the shorn lamb;" and in all His wonderful dispositions there is nothing so wonderful as this—that never was a soul left so utterly alone in its misery and hopelessness but succour could be found if it would stretch out its hand and take it. And, be again God thanked for it, many do. Pride may resist, the devil may argue that to retreat is impossible, human nature may pretend that the slavery is sweet. But the God of love is not beaten; in one way or another He stretches out His hand to His beloved. A friend passes by, and at once the loneliness is gone; a word of sympathy is uttered, and the barrier of silence is broken; a prayer is poured forth, from two hearts instead of one, and the grace is given that heals the wound. All these are there, if the poor, beaten soul will take them; if it only will!

"Peter going out wept bitterly." We are told that he wept for the remainder of his days. But surely the tears were not always bitter. Bitter tears are tears of remorse and unrepentance, of slavery to evil and inability to escape. But tears of repentance are solace to the soul, and fast grow to tears of love; and tears of love are sweet indeed. God is very good; He would not ever have any soul unhappy, not even the most stained; but He asks as the price of happiness that we should cling to Him, and not stab His own Heart to the quick. "Taste and see how sweet is the Lord." These are the words of a penitent; and they have been found by experience to be true by millions who have "lifted up their eyes to the mountains where dwelleth light."

There are many sorrows in this world, but no sorrow like to that of a soul that has fallen and refuses to rise. And there are many joys; but no joy can equal the joy of the soul that may have wandered a little, but at last leaps forward to the arms of its Father, and clings about His neck, and tells Him it has learnt its lesson, and that henceforth nothing shall tear it from His embrace. Such a soul is not the worse, but far the better for its bitter experience. It now knows what it did not know before; it now can help others in ways it never could have helped them otherwise; for that reason, perhaps, Peter was permitted to pass through the ordeal, and Paul and Augustine and many more. The school of bitter grief has been the school of Apostles; for they have learnt both the evil of sin, and the light and gladness and the liberating power of the love of God. "The wages of sin is death. But the grace of God life everlasting in Christ Jesus Our Lord."

Let the truth not be forgotten; there is no merit or greatness or goodness in submitting to misery, not even because of sin. But there is much merit and strength in the happy heart that clings to God our Lord, Who has a welcome for all, but for none more than for the sheep that strayed and has returned. "Rejoice with me," He says; and if my Father is happy in my return, then I will not spoil His happiness by being miserable myself.

# WOMAN

"It is not good for man to be alone; let us make him a help like unto himself."—Genesis ii. 18.

An English poet, in a poem familiar to us all, laments "to think what man has made of man." There is much truth in the poem; on the other hand there is much that is untrue; for in spite of all the harm that man has done to man, man is what he is by the help of his fellow-men, and man is on the whole a noble and a lovable creature. There is more good than evil in the world, more good than evil in man; and we need to keep this truth ever in our minds if we mean to judge life aright.

But perhaps the poet would have had more upon his side if he had sung, not of "what man has made of man," but of "what man has made of woman"; and perhaps more still if he had pondered on the counterpart of this, "what woman has made of man." This implies nothing against woman, for reverence of woman is ingrained in the present writer's mind, a gift to him from his mother; it only is a question, asking whether she who was made "like man, a help like unto man," has in matter of fact been a help to him or not. Certainly she has not been a help to him and nothing more; from the days of Eve herself there is a heavy charge against her; and one reflects with sadness on the judgment of a priest of fifty years' experience, that if women were what they should be men would be almost entirely good.

In truth the older one grows, and the more one has experience of mankind, the more does one recognise this fact; that most women, above all most young women, do not realise their proper dignity, do not realise their power, but play with the one and are reckless with the other until both slip from their grasp. Woman comes into the world, and grows up in the world, with all the dignity of a queen; her weakness is her defence, if only she will not throw away her shield; her honour is her admiration, if only she will not make light of it; her power over man is incalculable, if only she will not misuse it, if she will show in herself that she is worthy to wield it, if she will keep it true and not bend man by means of it to any selfish ends of her own. But too often woman awakens to all this when it is too late; she has revelled in the sunshine of her glory, laughed at the slavery she has enforced, until the sun has sunk, and the slave has revolted, and she is left alone, helpless in herself, useless to others, broken for the rest of her days.

For what is the secret of woman? What is that in her which draws human nature around her, and makes every woman a queen if she will be one? Too often she discovers it by experience, and is content with the fact; she does not look to its basis so that it may be made secure. But if she will examine her own heart she can very soon know. What is that which she respects most in herself; which, so long as she possesses it, she cherishes as a pearl beyond all price; which her first and last instinct, without any teaching or instruction, tells her is the first thing on which her dignity, and attraction, and her power lie?

We need not dig deep before we find our answer; it is written on the face of every true woman, found within her hand, stamped upon her very dress; and we call it her honour, because it is the noblest word we can find. A sinless woman, particularly in one respect, that is a thing before which all the world bows down; and if man desires to possess it, even if evil man is willing to destroy it, it is only because he knows that it is the greatest treasure on this earth. Sinlessness negative, which consists in freedom from stain; sinlessness positive, which will keep every danger of stain far from itself; this is the true secret of a woman's dignity, the root from which all true beauty and charm and personal fascination grow.

But sinlessness is kept in a frail vessel; and

that frail vessel is herself. To rob a woman of her honour directly and outright, the first time at least, is scarcely possible; that the "enemy of the human race" knows well, and those know it well who are his votaries. A thief will not enter by a door that is barred; he will not come before our very eyes; he will not bear about him the marks of his profession; rather he will find an open window, he will take you unawares, and if you chance to meet him he will declare he is that which he is not. So is the thief of the honour of woman, from the day of Eve till now; woman's weakest point is precisely that which in another sense is her strongest, the tendency to take that for good which is evil, to yield a little that greater good may come, to deceive even herself that she may attain "the knowledge of good and evil."

It is easy and alas! too common to have evidence of the process. A child steps into life with the brightness of her childhood upon her; thinking little of herself, because as yet she has not discovered herself, full of life, because inwardly serene, full of splendour and promise. Men look on and admire; as yet admiration is enough; though that very admiration means the beginning of her power. Which way will she use it?

Soon, very soon, she becomes conscious of it all. She can draw the eyes of men; she can

win the hearts of men; she can bend men to
obey her will; her presence or her absence
can even decide the happiness of many. It is
an intoxicating discovery; her cheek flushes,
her eyes are brighter, she holds her head
higher, she steps abroad more lightly, she
laughs at every fancy, a queen in her domain
of mankind. And if so much is good and
glorious, then why not more? If such is her
influence, why should it not be greater? Let
her go further and conquer for herself—she
may even whisper that she conquers for God
—all that will, nay must be for the best. So
she plunges in, laughingly, daringly, declar-
ing that she sees no harm, silencing every
warning, accustoming herself to every further
step, defying conscience until at last it ceases
to speak, making more and more merry on
the outside and telling herself that this is life,
allowing herself no time or thought to see
how it is within, refusing to believe what she
very well knows, or knew before she made
the plunge, that at the end of this road lies
the death of her best self and a heart-wound
for the remainder of her life.

> " She sang as she danced along the path,
>     An' the words came down to me :
> ' What matter a thought of the future years,
>     When love and youth are free ?'
> Singing she passed along the path
>     With myriad flowers entwined :
> Fairer her face than the days of spring,
>     But her eyes—oh ! her eyes were blind !"

I know I am speaking to deaf ears; that is the agony of the priest. One curls her lip in contempt, and says that of course a priest should speak like this; but he does not know life and its delights. Another is indignant and will have no interference; her soul, she says, and its salvation are her own affair. Yet a third cries out that so-and-so does this and is no worse for it, that thousands of others do the same; and why should not she be allowed to do likewise? A fourth, with a little tenderness left in her heart, listens to his words, and fears there may be something in them, but she fears no less to lose that intoxication of which she has begun to taste. And meanwhile to each and all the serpent whispers on, and the echo is repeated from countless mouths all around: "No, you shall not die the death. For God doth know that in what day soever you shall eat thereof, your eyes shall be opened; and you shall be as gods, knowing good and evil."

Yes, all this is spoken to deaf ears; once the path has been deliberately chosen it is hard to take a step back. The consent becomes a fascination, the fascination becomes a slavery; honour goes, dignity is lost; and the laughter of flattery that led the way, now that the poor victim lies in the mire robbed of both, turns into the laughter of contempt. She was our queen, now she is our slave; before she commanded, now she is wholly at our mercy; at one time she had power to lead us to good, she has used her power to do harm, and let her take the consequences. And those who know only too well where all this wildness leads, can do no more than look on, and utter their vain appeal, and pray God to have mercy at least in the end.

And it might have been so different. Woman is made to help man, not to lead him to his ruin; and man is made to cherish the good that is in woman, not to drag her into worse than death. Oh! children, yet unspoilt, young women yet but awakening to life, mothers who have your daughters' integrity at heart, remember that woman is at once stronger than man and weaker; stronger in her instincts for all that is best, weaker in her yielding nature; stronger perhaps in her sympathies, weaker against fascination. Remember this, and as you value your lives, as you value your dignity, your honour, your power for doing good, cultivate your strength, beware of your weakness; believe not the serpent, or his human counterpart, who tells you that your strength is your weakness, your weakness your strength.

If only one ear would listen and be warned in time, and would not be "wise in its own conceit"! For that we will gladly endure the sneer and contempt of many.

# COURAGE

If there is one thing more than another that a man most aspires to be esteemed for it is his courage. If there is one thing more than another that a woman most admires in a man it is his courage. If in a woman there is one thing more valued than another, it is that quiet courage which goes by many names—endurance, patience, loyalty, consistency with truth, willingness to face whatever lies before her. Nor is there much to choose between man's courage and the courage of woman. If man has the courage of physical action, woman has the greater courage of privation; and on the other hand, if man has less courage to submit to being thwarted, when woman is defeated, and has to rise again, her courage tends to fail her utterly. Both have their strong points, both their limitations; but in both alike the greatest courage of all is to fight up against their weakest nature.

It will not be denied by many that bravery in ordinary life means the power to face and to go through hard things; cowardice in practice means the shirking of a duty. It does not matter much what excuses we may make, to what subterfuges we may resort, how successfully we may deceive ourselves or others. Let the outward show of things be what it may, the man who always takes the easiest line of life, and who always finds reasons, justifications, for taking the easiest line of life, no matter how brave, and grand, and assertive those reasons may sound, is in the end no more than a coward; the modern popular affectation of a square jaw and an unbending eye, cultivated nowadays so assiduously, will not save him from self-condemnation. On the other hand the man who does the right thing, or, harder still, having done the wrong thing owns up to it, and makes an effort to put it right or atone for it, is a brave man, no matter what it may cost him, and no matter what others may think; indeed, the more it costs him, and the more he has public opinion to face, the braver man he must be said to be.

Now there are various ways of facing an unpleasant and difficult situation, but three are by far the most common. One is to face it and not to look at it; to pretend to oneself that it does not exist; to put on a smile outside and hide the consciousness beneath so far as one is able; to affect bravery, all the more because one is a shirker. For instance, it is far easier, when one has done an evil deed, to deny that the deed is evil, than to repent of the evil that is done; and there are very many cowards who hide themselves beneath that sham. To say: "It is not wrong," when one knows very well that it is, is characteristic of a coward; such a man, with all his show of daring, is really afraid, afraid of himself, afraid of others, afraid of the consequences of repentance. Morally such a man is of the type of those sham gentlemen of paper collars, and paste diamonds, and empty pockets, whose one object in life is to make people believe they are what they are not. Such men are very common, more common than they like to think themselves; by being at once so common and so shallow they are easily known by the discerning; if they only knew how easily they were known perhaps they would strut a little less in their garb of sham morality.

The second class is more common still, but is yet more difficult to discern; it is the class of those who, with the situation before them, make up their minds that they will live two lives. A man has done evil; the evil has entered into his life; it has become part of himself in so far as he has told himself that he can no longer do without it. He is at least braver than the first type of person, who is unwilling to acknowledge the evil he has done; at least he owns in his own heart what duty dictates, even though he tells himself that he cannot obey. The fascination holds him; to make a clean breast of it and begin again is more than he can endure; he must carry his burden in secret, and put on without as bold a face as he is able.

So the double life begins; outside "whited sepulchres, but within rottenness and dead men's bones"; and how many there are who go to their graves smiling and esteemed, honoured by men for their uprightness and courage; yet have been to themselves things of utter contempt, and have dragged a weary burden behind them all their lives! One act of courage, and all might have been so different; then there would have been no need for endless counterfeiting. Only one act of courage, following on the courage of clear understanding; and yet that one act—what an effort, for some, it implies! They prefer the burden and its consequences, no matter what the weight.

But there is a third class of moral coward, and this is the worst of all. The first one can despise, because it is dishonest to itself; the man who will affect to see no evil in evil doing, merely that he may save himself the trouble of avoiding it, is his own worst enemy and may simply be set aside. The second class one pities; one longs to help him; if he has not the courage to do what he ought, his weakness is after all one that belongs to human nature. But with the third class one is indignant, because it is the most inhuman; it is the class of those who have substituted brazenness for bravery. We all know the crew, but we do not always know its individual members, so clever are they in the art of confounding one kind of bravery with another. A man has done wrong; he knows that to evade it, and to declare it to be no evil, is merely contemptible; he himself scorns the evildoer who adopts this device. He knows, too, that to own the wrong, and yet to fret beneath its burden, is pitiable; he has no part with those who so compel themselves to lead two lives.

Braver is it, he tells himself, if he has done wrong, to live up to it. If he has done wrong, why then he has done so; and wrong-doing is a sign of a man of courage. He has deeply wronged another; such wrong-doing, he will boldly say, is but a proof of his manly vigour. His poor victim in his clutches makes a life-and-death struggle to recover; it is laughed at for its timidity, it is abused for its disloyalty, it is harrassed and thwarted at every turn, taunted to be "brave" and keep itself free from priest-craft and conscience, told that it must, if it would enjoy life, defy alike God, man, and devil. He will have none of your womanish priests to interfere with his "manly" ways; none of your milk-sop pious people, who have not the "courage" to sin like himself; none of your chicken-hearted lovers of righteousness, who will not let them-

selves "enjoy" life like himself. "I have
sinned, and what harm has befallen me?" he
cries with the sinner in the Scripture; and he
holds up his head, and struts through life, "a
law unto himself," the first principle of which
is that sin is a mark of courage.

When we look at the dealings of Jesus
Christ with men, it is easy to see how He
singles out this third class for His most
emphatic condemnation. For the merely blind
He prays: "Father, forgive them, for they
know not what they do;" and that even though
their blindness is chiefly from themselves. For
the weak He holds out a helping hand; even
Judas, the finally impenitent traitor, He treats
with pity to the end; for even Judas owned
that he "had sinned." But for these other
cowards, these cowards who hid their nature
under the garb of brazenness, who sinned,
and "braved" it, and taught it to others, for
these He has only indignation and doom.

"He who receiveth one tiny child in my
name, receiveth Me. But he who shall scan-
dalise one of these tiny children who believe in
Me, it were better for him that a mill-stone
were tied about his neck and that he were cast
into the depths of the sea. Woe to the world
because of scandals! It must needs be that
scandal should come. But woe to that man
by whom the scandal cometh." For the rest
of men, Jesus Christ tells us, He prays; for

such as these He does not pray; for He leaves them to their self-inflicted sentence.

No, if we understand aright, we shall see that this type condemns itself. For courage, as we have acknowledged at the outset of this essay, is the power to face and go through with things that are hard; to shirk a duty, on whatever plea, is always the mark of a coward. To have done wrong and not to own it, that so one may escape the consequent repentance, is cowardice and nothing more. To have done wrong and to acknowledge it, yet to leave it unatoned for and unhealed, is cowardice of another kind, more pitiful perhaps than the first but no less real. But to have done wrong, and to acknowledge it, and then to "brave it out" with arrogance, and mockery, and laughter; to break the law and to teach the same to others by word, and example, and compulsion; that is the greatest cowardice of all. And it meets with a coward's doom, not only in the next life but even in this; for such a man, despite the din and recklessness around him, is devoid of friends, has killed all human sympathy, and when his day is ended there will not be one who will feel that the world is the poorer for his loss.

# THE LAY APOSTOLATE

It is the inevitable consequence of the democratic age in which we live that everything, education, government, even religion, should fall into the hands of the people. There must still be school-masters, but the people will decide what shall be taught. There must still be ministers to frame and to pass laws, but the people must tell them what those laws shall be, and see to their fulfilment. And in religion there must still be priests and bishops; there must still be all that inherited possession which no revolution can destroy; but the working element of the faith, the preservation of the faith, the spread of the faith, the manifestation of the faith to men, all this, from the very nature of the case, must devolve more and more upon the people. If the people do their duty then religion will be safe, will go forward and prosper, no matter what else may happen; if they are wanting, then no amount of preaching by its priests, or of administration by its ministers, will save it from failure.

Of course in some sense this has been always true; but it has never been more true than now, unless we except the very first ages of the Church. Then, too, she depended, per-

haps more than on anything else, on the prac
tice and example of her children.  Without
that, as St. Paul, St. Peter, St. James, and
St. John so often hint, all preaching would be
in vain; with it, then apostles might be put to
death, bishops and popes might be exiled and
imprisoned, but for all that the Church would
conquer the world.  For that was a people's
world, and the Church was a people's Church;
and if the people were worthy of the Church
then the world was hers.  So is it in our day;
the people own the world in a very real sense
in this generation, and they, and almost they
alone, can decide in what state the future of
the Church shall be.  More than prelates,
more than priests and apostles and preachers,
they can spread her cause or can condemn her
to yet further subjection.

For this reason it behoves us to look about
and bestir ourselves.  If so much lies with us,
if this is one among the many consequences of
our hardly-earned liberty, then it behoves us
to accept it and to use it well.  For every gift
of liberty brings with it a corresponding duty;
if I am to be worthy of the one I must look to
the other.  What then is imposed upon me?
Am I to turn missioner and preacher?  Am I
to become an exponent of the Church and her
teaching?  Am I to put religion in the first
place in my life, and make all the rest revolve
round it?  Does this entail for me the sacri-

fice of myself or of the things that are mine; of my family, my friends, my pleasures, my relaxations, my interests? Or if not, what exactly is meant by, and what is the limit of, this responsibility which has come to me? For if the gaining of freedom, which is the conquest of this generation, means all this, then it would seem to be but the exchanging of one kind of subjection for another.

Let us try to answer this enquiry in as few words as possible. To begin with, there are some for whom this responsibility may indeed mean all that has just been asked. Some may feel and know in their hearts that they are asked to prove their freedom, and their right use of it, by freely surrendering it; as many a rich man feels that he then makes the best use of his riches when he gives it away. Such men know beyond a doubt that nothing else but this complete surrender of themselves will satisfy them; by no other course of action will they be happy. But these are by no means all; they are the very few; they are those of whom we say that they have a vocation, for a vocation in this limited and accepted sense is defined as a call to devote oneself entirely to the work of God.

Of these, then, and to these we do not here speak. We speak rather to those to whom we can say at once that the responsibility of their freedom does not exact so much. How much, then, it will be asked, does it exact? I do not know; it will differ in each case; but in general it may be said to be as much as an able and willing heart is able and willing to give. Circumstances are to be considered; individual characters are to be considered. A married man, with family cares, and other anxieties, cannot always give as much as one who has but himself to look to; a married woman usually still less. Again a character that is naturally shy, and reserved, and contemplative can often make itself do less than one that is by nature open, and expansive, and active; all this must be taken into account when we make our estimates.

These things presupposed, let us now descend to something very practical. To begin with there is one thing, and after all the one important thing, for the spread of the Church which every man can do. He can look to himself; he can set a good example; conscious as he is that wherever he goes he carries the honour of the Church with him, he can look to it that that honour is not tarnished. Such a man will in public and before others do nothing that is unworthy of a member of the Church; such a man will do everything which is expected of him; if he has power over others, he will do what in him lies to see that they too are worthy of the Church to which they belong. By such means was Christianity mainly spread at the beginning; by such means is it being spread to-day; though—alas! that we should have to say it—it is because of the neglect of this first duty among those who bear its name that Christianity in many places fails and falters.

But there are many who can say with the young man in the Gospel: "This I have observed from my youth; what else can I do?" For these, then, let us see whether we can make any suggestions. There are few who, if they will look about them, will not find abundant opportunities of doing good. There are our own subjects of one kind or another; these, in a quiet but unassuming way, we can influence more than we do, to think and act in the right direction. There are our own friends and equals; these, by some kind of co-operation, we can turn into towers of strength. There are the poor about us, whom we have always with us; and by the poor we do not merely mean those who are in need of money. We can, if we will, lend a helping hand in many places where help is needed; we can give much more than mere gold and silver. I once knew a man who made a rule for himself to spend an hour every day if he could in doing something for somebody; and wonderful were the devices he discovered for making himself useful.

In this lies the principle; its application may be very varied. Let us see. In France and

some parts of England, it is common to find a
man or woman offer their services to their
parish priest to give instructions. Some will
instruct children, some will instruct the grown-
ups who are ignorant, some will instruct con-
verts. In France and England, again, the
practice is growing for men, and sometimes
women, to see to it that young people after
leaving school do not fall away from the faith.
They follow them up; they see that they go
to the sacraments; they support the clubs and
gatherings instituted for their use. In Italy
and Spain, in England, France, and North
America, young men work hard among themselves for their own training. They study
social questions, they meet for discussion, they
write essays, at times there will appear in some
paper or review a telling essay, the fruit of
their re-unions. Then there is the spreading
of good literature. In many ways may this be
done. There are the regular Catholic papers,
there is an ever-growing output of Catholic
books; if only our laymen and women would
work for the circulation of these, what a world
of good they would be doing!

Again, there is a kind of good work which,
one has reason to fear, is very much neglected
in these days. It is true one sometimes does
find ladies visiting hospitals, refuges, and even
prisons; one sometimes finds there Salvation
Army officers; but how seldom does one find

our own men! And yet why should it not be possible for them to do good work there as well as for anyone else? A man can smooth a pillow, a man can light a cigarette, a man can wash a hand or a face, a man can write a letter, a man can lift a patient, a man can bring a cheering book or paper—and a man can encourage a back-slider to lift up his face to God, and determine to reform his life and begin again. And to the man who will attempt it I can promise one thing; he will find it engrossingly interesting. He will find a new meaning in life. He will understand life as he has never understood it before, that is, from many points of view besides his own

These, then, are some of the ways by which we can make the lay apostolate a real thing; there are many more, which a soul that is keen will not fail to discover. Only let us set to work and something will be done. Let us work together and then, as our Lord has promised: "Where there are two or three gathered together in my name there am I in the midst of them." If we want further encouragement, let us remember the words of St. James: "He who causeth a sinner to be converted from the error of his way, shall save his own soul from death, and shall cover a multitude of sins." And those other words of Our Lord Himself: "Come, ye blessed of my Father, possess the kingdom prepared for you from the foundation of the world. For I was hungry, and you gave me to eat: I was thirsty, and you gave me to drink; I was a stranger, and you took me in; naked, and you covered me; sick, and you visited me; I was in prison, and you came to me." For " Amen I say to you, as long as you did it to one of these my least brethren, you did it to me."

# THE SCHOOL OF LOVE

"BE zealous for the better gifts," says St. Paul in a well-known passage. "And I shew unto you yet a more excellent way." Then the apostle breaks out into that wonderful description of love, which has been worn threadbare by all writers and preachers; worn threadbare, and yet it is ever new, ever thrilling, ever inspiring. "Love is patient, is kind. Love envieth not, dealeth not perversely; is not puffed up, is not ambitious, seeketh not her own, is not provoked to anger, thinketh no evil, rejoiceth not in iniquity, but rejoiceth with the truth; beareth all things, believeth all things, hopeth all things, endureth all things. Love never falleth away. . . . Follow after love" (1 Cor. xiii.).

Love is a word we play with very easily. We use it for the most trifling emotions; we even use it with a sense of evil, so that we almost fear to have it on our lips at all, lest others take scandal at our language. Nevertheless the word is the greatest and the deepest that human tongue has ever invented. It is almost too deep for definition. Poets have extolled it from the beginning of the world; philosophers have discussed and analysed it; men and women have lived for it and died for it by millions; upon it man builds up this existence, and God Himself has built eternity; it is the key to this life, the content of the next, the abiding link between both, the mortal's possession that can never die, the fire of life that leaps across the chasm made by death.

Love, then, almost laughs at definition. It is too vivid, too burning a thing to be defined; if it could be adequately defined—no doubt it can—it would still have no meaning for us, it would almost appear contemptible, unless we ourselves had known it by our own experience. A man understands what love is, and has love in him, in so far as he has himself actually loved, and does love, and no further. Philosophy will not teach him the real thing; poetry will not help him much; when he has felt it, and has been stirred by it, and has longed, at least, and striven, to be something and to do something because of it, then, and to that extent, he will know it. He will know, too, that he has not reached its end; that there are other depths of love to which he has not yet attained. He may reach to them some day; meanwhile it is something to have discovered what he knows.

Hence, for the understanding of love, it is more important to describe than to define it;

to see it in its effects rather than on paper;
to watch it in its growth and making, that so,
if we really wish for it ourselves, we may
follow the path that leads towards it. And
the key to it is given to us in the very simple
words of one who certainly knew.

"Love," says a certain great master of the
science, "is seen in deeds rather than in
words." That is the key to the whole matter:
the deeds that love will make us do. Let us,
then, watch love in action; above all, let us
watch it as it beats against the bars of its
prison within our own hearts. For it is there
most of all, perhaps there only, that we can
read it securely for ourselves, and according
to the measure of our own capacity, without
any fear of being misled, without any danger
of getting out of our depth. "The kingdom
of God," said our Lord, "is within you;" and
the kingdom of God is nothing if not the
kingdom of Love.

What, then, do I understand by a loving
nature, the good ground on which the seed of
love is likely to bear most abundant fruit?
I understand, first of all, a nature that is easily
led to think little of itself. It is a nature
which, as it were, is easily distracted from itself by appreciation and admiration of that
which it finds around it and in others. Outside itself it is for ever discovering matter of
interest, something worth attention, so that

to itself it forgets to give much thought. Such
a trait is common in children, and we love
them for it. To them, until they are spoilt,
all the world is new and wonderful; themselves they have not yet discovered. We see
it in great poets and great artists. Love of
that which inspires them is their life; it makes
them unlike other men, act unlike other men,
and the common human nature that is in us
all makes us claim for them forgiveness for
much excess because we know they have
loved much.

Secondly, by a loving nature I understand
a nature of deep emotions. Not merely does
it see and appreciate; it is affected by its
appreciations, it suffers one way or another.
There are some natures that fall short of this;
they can appreciate the beautiful, they can
analyse it, they can describe it, in some sense
they can be interested in it, but to be moved
by it in any undue degree would seem to them
a weakness. Such natures may attain to
much more, especially by way of intellect; but
if emotion does not follow, their love is a
crippled thing. Love feels joy, love feels
sorrow. When it joys, its joy may swell till
it becomes an agony, and it is compelled to
cry out: "No more, no more!" When it
sorrows, its sorrow may be worse than death,
and yet it will cherish it with a sense of nature
satisfied. When it has neither joy nor sorrow,

then, whatever else there may be, life is like
an empty desert.

Thirdly, by a loving nature I understand a
nature that can act. True love demands a
certain courage, a certain daring, to act not
merely by the dictate of reason, but also by
the prompting of love. True, it is liable to
make mistakes; it may be convicted of much
foolishness, of many excesses of generosity.
Love does not always calculate, does not always
consider pros and cons, is not always prudent
as some philosophers understand that virtue,
does not always look for success, but, once
aroused, shuts its eyes, "gives and does not
count the cost, fights and does not heed the
wounds, toils and does not seek for rest,
labours and looks for no reward," lays down
its life and does not think about it. Such a
nature is dangerous? Yes; but it is dangerous
to go into battle; it is dangerous to go out
upon the mission field; it is dangerous to tend
the diseased; it is of the essence of all greatness to face what is dangerous. "Greater
love than this no man hath, that he lay down
his life for his beloved," whoever or whatever
that beloved may be.

Such is a loving nature, as it comes from the
hand of God: the development of that nature
is the meaning of this life. It may be cultivated and fostered so that it may become
capable of ever more and more; it may be

clipped and dwarfed so that in the end it droops into a pitiable weed; it may be grown on artificial lines, pruned into a caricature of nature, so that it develops like those box-wood or yew-tree imitations of birds, or animals, or chairs, which in an artificial age were once thought to be beautiful.

And if it may be cultivated, then obviously it will be along the three lines which have been already pointed out. If true love is disinterested, then he who would cultivate the power of loving will cultivate disinterestedness. If true love is moved by strong emotion, then the devotee of love will let himself be drawn by emotion as well as by reason, however much reason may hold the reins; will not submit to be imprisoned in his own shallow argumentation narrowed down by his own blinking vision; will overleap himself in his esteem of and longing for objects more precious than himself. Lastly, and consequently, the man who would truly love, and know to the full what it means, will beware of that timid limping thing which sometimes parades, and hides its littleness, under the name of prudence. He will have a large horizon, reaching out beyond the range of life. He will learn the art of giving, with a hand outspread, as if all he had were but for this purpose. He will live with a large and unflinching generosity, revelling in the freedom from pettiness of whatever kind, "envying not, dealing not perversely, seeking not his own," but always "rejoicing with the truth." This is the atmosphere in which love grows.

In the same way may I test and examine such degree of love as I possess; for little as it is, that it is none I will not allow. St. Teresa once described hell as "the place where there is no love"; and in spite of all its miseries my soul has not yet come to that. Crawling and bleeding though it be from many wounds, there is yet life in it; and if life, then love. But has that love grown straight or crooked? Is it growing straight or crooked now? Is it wholly true, or is it partly true and partly false? And if the latter, is the false so growing on the true that the flower is becoming blighted, the fruit rotting at the core, however fair it may seem without? Let us see.

If what has been said is sound, then the less my love has a thought for itself so much the more true it is. It seeks not its own, it is not for mere pleasure that it loves; nor for the pleasurable consequences, unless it be the joy of its nature fulfilled, the joy of giving and of sacrifice. Sweetness indeed may be there, and sweetness of such kind as alone deserves the name. But not on its account is love pursued; to pursue it for its sake is the throttling of love, making it a slave instead of a master, using it for some other end, when it is itself the noblest and only end of all. Is my love of this calibre?

Secondly, if my love does not stir me, or stirs me but a very little, less than many other motives which make their impress on me, then is it tending to die. A stoic, ancient or modern, who boasts of being above emotion, who acts by his reason and that only, who prides himself on doing his duty, has triumphed over love, scotched it if he has not killed it; it is a gruesome triumph, the triumph of the polar ice over the underlying land. Beauty there may be of a kind, beauty, and strength, and stillness; but life, and warmth, and growth, and fruitfulness there can be none. But love stirs all the strings upon the human heart; sometimes, even, it sweeps its master-hand across them and stirs them all together so that the poor, dear, enviable human creature is all joy and all agony at once. Because they are not its own, because they are the joys and the sorrows of others, they are multiplied beyond control, each beating up against the other, sometimes in harmony, sometimes in discord, but always throbbing with a sympathy that others instinctively detect; till at last the poor, loving heart does not know itself, does not know whether to call itself happy or distressed, tossed as it is upon the billows of emotion, torn by the cries, scorched by the tears, of all the creatures it loves, wonders at itself and its capacity for suffering, asks itself, trembling, whether after all it has chosen the right path, is consoled by nothing that others understand by consolation, and sees only death as its escape from the whirl and tangle of emotion. To how many lives of loving saints is not this the key? Is it not the key to the Heart of Christ Himself, and to His agony in the garden? Is it the key to my heart?

Thirdly, love is a restless thing. Idleness and love are incompatible; love cannot go to sleep. This does not necessarily mean the activity that men usually understand; it need not be doing anything; but it means that it is ever awake and on fire within the depths of its own heart. What it can give it gives; it longs to give what it cannot; it bankrupts itself, and counts its bankruptcy gain; it glories in so having nothing, for the very having nothing proves that it is master of all. "The kingdom of heaven is likened to a treasure hidden in a field. Which a man having found, hid it, and for joy thereof goeth, and selleth all that he hath, and buyeth that field. Again the kingdom of heaven is like to a merchant seeking good pearls. Who when he had found one pearl of great price, went his way, and sold all that he had, and bought it."

Of course this does not mean that love leads inevitably to poverty. Sometimes it does; sometimes it demands a surrender even of the things of earth. A husband gives all to his wife, a wife to her husband; many a man has beggared himself for love of a noble cause. Still these are but the trappings of love, which may or may not be present; a millionaire can love as well as a pauper; where love leads a pauper can give as much as a millionaire. For it is the gift of oneself that matters; the gift of a human heart, its homage, its reverence, its service, the outpouring of itself, in whatever condition it may be placed, the giving of its life, whether that life is destined to live on or is demanded as a present sacrifice. "Christ loved me, and gave Himself for me," says St. Paul dumbfounded at the holocaust; and he answers with an eloquence that will hardly find its match in literature: "I am sure that neither death, nor life, nor angels, nor principalities, nor powers, nor things present, nor things to come, nor might, nor height, nor depth, nor any other creature shall be able to separate us from the love of God, which is in Christ Jesus our Lord."

So does true love impel; love impels to love; love impelled to love has love for its reward; its beginning and its end is only love. Is my love of this nature? For this is the third and final test.

Yes, as we have already said, when we look at love aright we see that to love demands great courage. To love perfectly is the greatest heroism; even lesser heroism is what it is because of the love that inspires it. There is something terrible in love. It is exacting, it is almost merciless; it will have the whole or nothing; above all it will have no rapine in the holocaust; it will abide no giving with one hand, and taking back with the other. If you would love well and deeply you must be prepared to lose; to "lay down your life for your friend"; and to lay down if need be everything that is of less moment than life. What in matter of fact you may be asked for you do not know. It may be the laying down of life; it may be the taking of it up. It may be the torture of wounds; it may perhaps be the greater torture of ministering to the wounds of others. It may be action, it may be its opposite, inaction and endurance

"Those also serve who only stand and wait." But undoubtedly it will be something, and you will not be consulted as to what it shall be.

Does the prospect appal you? If it does, very well; but be assured there is no other road to the real understanding of love. If it does not, if in spite of the dread there is still hope and courage, if you can still say that love can find strength to do whatever love may demand, if you would know by experience the meaning of love, then make your preparations. Put a check upon self-seeking, on self-gratification, on looking for self-reward, and you have cleared the ground. Be led by something more than mere argument, mere reasoning of your own, that dead and fallacious thing that is the offspring of man's short sight; see without turning aside, submit to without drawing back, be guided by without flinching, the compelling force of truth in itself, of nobility in itself, of beauty in itself, of goodness in itself, wherever these may be found. And lastly, when the spirit is moved to act, to give itself for something noble, to follow the light, to do that which is in itself worth doing, then let it go. Do not hesitate; do not keep it in fetters; do not too much count the cost; do not tremble at the danger; or if you do, for you cannot always help it, set your teeth and step forward. "He that putteth his hand to the plough and looketh back, is not worthy of me."

These are the exercises by which the power to love may be developed. On such ground, under such training, love will grow; of that you need not doubt. For the germ of love is in every human heart; the pity of it is that in some it is nipped and frost-bitten before it has had time to come to maturity. But foster the spark and it will enkindle. At first it will thrill you with its glow. You will know it by its heat, by the ease with which it aids you to face a trouble, by the joy you find in doing. But later, be prepared for sacrifice. When the flower has bloomed and the fruit is setting, then, gardeners tell us, is the time of trial. When you have made a certain way, and you have laughed and sung along the road, then will love begin to lead through darker ways, and whither you would not; it will ask of you surrenders for which you had not bargained. It will disappoint you; it will fail to recognise you when you come face to face; it will leave your noblest actions unrequited, the noblest powers of your soul undeveloped. It will misinterpret your best motives, will envy your worthiest deeds, will crush you with sarcasm, will embitter you with mistrust, and suspicion, and dislike, and an assumption of contempt. At critical moments it will turn its back upon you, will ignore you when you are down, if you appeal for help will cry out against you. It will see you wounded on the road and pass you by; crucified, and say it was only your desert; dripping your life's blood out, and coldly wait the end.

And then, when it has killed you, then you will come to know. "He that loses his life for my sake shall find it." When it has purified you, when there is left not a spark of that mean thing self, when you no longer look for relief, for consolation, for comfort, but only for strength to go on, then will come the revelation. Then you will know that which, by any other training, eye can never see, nor ear hear, nor can it enter into the heart of man to conceive.

# Uniform with this Volume

**THE CONTEMPLATIVE LIFE.** Considered in its Apostolic Aspect. By a Carthusian Monk. With Frontispiece.

**THE CROWN OF SORROW.** By Archbishop Goodier, S.J.

**THE CRUCIFIX; OR, PIOUS MEDITATIONS.** From the French. 2nd Edition. With Frontispiece.

**DANGERS OF THE DAY.** By Bishop Vaughan. With Portrait.

**A DOCTRINE OF HOPE.** Adapted from a Pastoral Letter of Bishop Bonomelli. With an Introduction by Rev. C. C. Martindale, S.J.

**THE FRIAR PREACHER, YESTERDAY AND TO-DAY.** By Père Jacquin, O.P. Edited by Very Rev. Hugh Pope, O.P., S.T.M. With Frontispiece.

**FROM BETHLEHEM TO CALVARY.** Meditations on the Life of Our Lord, for Young People. By Mrs. Abel Ram. 3rd Edition.

**JESUS AMABILIS.** A Book for Daily Prayer. Compiled by Francesca Glazier.

**JESUS CHRIST THE SON OF GOD.** By Archbishop Goodier, S.J.

**THE LIFE OF UNION WITH OUR DIVINE LORD.** By Abbé F. Maucourant. 2nd Edition.

**A LITTLE BOOK OF ETERNAL WISDOM.** By Blessed Henry Suso, O.P. To which is added the celebrated "Parable of a Pilgrim." By Walter Hilton. New Edition.

**LOVE, PEACE, AND JOY.** A Month of the Sacred Heart, according to St. Gertrude. By Very Rev. André Prévot. 2nd Edition.

**THE MEANING OF LIFE, AND OTHER ESSAYS.** By Archbishop Goodier, S.J. 2nd Edition.

**THE PARABLES OF JESUS.** By Very Rev. Philip Coghlan, C.P.

**THE PASSION AND DEATH OF JESUS.** By Very Rev. Philip Coghlan, C.P.

**THE PRINCE OF PEACE.** A Series of Meditations by Archbishop Goodier, S.J., Author of "The Meaning of Life," etc.

**SANCTUARY.** By Mary Angela Dickens. Preface by Fr. Charles Galton, S.J. With Frontispiece.

**A SHORT METHOD OF MENTAL PRAYER.** By Most Rev. Nicholas Ridolfi. Translated into English by Fr. Raymund Devas, O.P.

**SIMPLICITY, ACCORDING TO THE GOSPEL.** By Mgr de Gibergues, Bishop of Valence. Author of "Faith," etc. With Frontispiece.